AMERICAN RENDERING

Books by Andrew Hudgins

AMERICAN RENDERING

NEW AND SELECTED POEMS

Andrew Hudgins

HOUGHTON MIFFLIN HARCOURT
BOSTON   NEW YORK
2010

www.hmhbooks.com

Library of Congress Cataloging-in-Publication Data
Hudgins, Andrew.
American rendering : new and selected poems / Andrew Hudgins.
p.   cm.
ISBN 978-0-547-24962-9
I. Title.
PS3558.U288A83 2010
811'.54 — dc22   2009029079

Book design by Brian Moore

Printed in the United States of America

DOC 10 9 8 7 6 5 4 3 2 1

FOR ERIN

Good and evill we know in the field of this World grow up together almost inseparably; and the knowledge of good is so involv'd and interwoven with the knowledge of evill, and in so many cunning resemblances hardly to be discern'd, that those confused seeds which were impos'd on Psyche as an incessant labour to cull out, and sort asunder, were not more intermixt. It was from out the rinde of one apple tasted, that the knowledge of good and evill as two twins cleaving together leapt forth into the World. And perhaps this is that doom which Adam fell into of knowing good and evill, that is to say of knowing good by evill. As therefore the state of man now is; what wisdome can there be to choose, what continence to forbeare without the knowledge of evill?

—JOHN MILTON, "AREOPAGITICA"

Contents

NEW POEMS

My Daughter

After midnight, I dragged carpet padding
from a trash bin and spread it on the asphalt
between the wall and dumpster. Screened from sleet,
I pulled carpet remnants over me, and that night
I married, raised a family, and outlived everyone
except a daughter — a teacher — and her two children,
one damaged. I woke when a bread truck scraped the bin.
From under damp carpet, I watched punctilious men
sign invoices, sweep, hose down the docks. A boy
in a bloody butcher's smock leaned against the wall
and smoked through bloody fingers.
                                        At night, I search
and sometimes find my daughter. "I make good money now,"
I tell her. "Let me take Teresa home with me.
I can buy the help she needs." My daughter smiles,
asks how I'm doing, and I lose the moment
to my wife, my job, my actual
family, as the thick-faced infant bucks in her arms
or beats her forehead hard and almost musically
against the table. When I clench her to my belly,
she screams, red-faced and rigid. "Hush, hush, hush,"
I serenade her. "O unhushable baby, hush."

Mother

Down the long, wide, and closely trimmed acres of Mammon,
plate toppling with saffron potato salad, I followed my shadow
to an appealingly dilapidated pond. Ghostly koi coasted under ripples
undulating to the tempo of hidden pumps. Fish mouths
mouthed my shadow, and among them moved a golden
adumbration. Voluptuous fins feathered the water, blossoming
like massive chrysanthemums that opened and opened
— bud to blowsy, blowsy to blown — and gently closed.
Gold propelled itself on delicate explosions, dissolving
and resolving in aureate metamorphoses, golden fish to golden flower,
flower to fish. But fins I thought petals were actually,
I could not believe this, wings. It was a trained bird, a pullet,
slipping under silk lilies. Before I could even be astonished,
the shadow of wealth stood beside my shadow, a large man,
sly look worn always openly. "I call that one Mother," he said,
and laughed. "Then I'll call her Mother too," I answered, laughing with him
because on Fridays I gathered balls while he snapped chip shots,
one after one, over the hood of his Benz, yellow balls
arcing black lacquer I'd polished and onto a green I'd swept.
He never thwacked a door panel, dimpled the hood, or, dear God,
as I prayed from behind a rigid grin, slapped a frosted star
through safety glass. "Risk," he explained. "Risk makes you concentrate."
Orange carp gulped hopefully at our reflections. A sandblasted dolphin,
nearly amorphous with calculated age, shot filtered water into filtered water.
"This is America," he told me. Though I was the help, of course I was invited.
At our feet, Mother, never surfacing, lapped the pool like an Olympian.

Accelerator

The man in front of us leaned out his door
and spat. The radio boohooed,
"I'm wearing my crying shoes." What the hell
does that mean? I wondered, as the blonde beside me,
eyes shut, heels propped on the dash, slapped her thighs,
and bawled, "Crying shoes! I'm wearing
my crying shoes."
                           "This light's going to last forever,"
I said. "Let's steal a car!" she answered, eyes glistening.
Scuffed bucks rested on the drilled-out brake
and accelerator. They were my shoes. I had a car. We were *in* it.
Or was that her point — I was boredom itself?
The spitter wheeled into Burger King, stood,
and, one hand on the roof, spat compactly,
watching it. "Steal a car? How about a movie?"
"What are you, the only white man left in the world?"
"No, there's me and whoever's singing that goddamn song.
And that dude spitting on his shoes. But that's it.
That's all of us." Violins slid in lard across the song's
sad bridge, and true to spoony music's low
simpering allure, I hummed along in her silence
until, with my right crying shoe, I pegged the accelerator.
The tires rose on haggard rubber, screaming
against the engine's scream, one song obliterating the other,
and the V-8 forging forward banged us back.

Lorraine's Song

Lorraine sang, *Mouth or knife,*
mouth or knife at
the knothole — which, which, which?
From the other side of the fence,
she sang, *Steel or lips*
at the knothole? Tongue
or blade? she chanted — *which,*
which, which, and giggled,
teasing. I put myself
in the hole. Myself? It felt
like my whole self when
she put her mouth on me
and I jerked away, afraid.
Bodiless laughter rang
from the opening, low and joyous.
Mouth or knife. Mouth
or knife. Which, which, which?

Walking a True Line

Red lights whirling behind her in the sun,
a cop ordered me off the trestle. *Why?*
I asked, squinting. I knew what she'd say.
I loved this shortcut to my bad job, loved walking
above the street and then above the river,
mincing across the slick, splintering ties
— a true line against a hard blue sky —
teasing a fear of heights with a love of rivers.
The trains don't use it anymore, I called
down to the voice that yelled what authority
must yell: "Get down anyway!" What
a surety the State was — Mom, with a holstered
nine millimeter.
                    That evening, as I trudged,
obeisant, below the trestle, giving Mom
time to forget, the creosoted posts,
oozing tar, shuddered like oracles.
Above, unseen, a lugubrious chugging mass
passed over, painstakingly, almost half aware,
as gods proceed when they think they love us,
we who are in this world to be swept away.

Everything Before "Happy" Is True

Mrs. Richey manned the big desk, marking quizzes,
my little desk pulled next to hers like a tender
moored in the lee of a dreadnought holed
below the waterline, while I sidled fearfully through rows
of students crooked by the state over the State's
disfigured books, laboring toward the past-
perfect tense. "Is that past-perfect or simply the past?"
I asked again and again until a boy, sick of hearing it,
backhanded me across the neck. I caught my fall
against a thickset girl, who snarled, "Get
your hands off me, white man!"
                                    When I jerked upright,
he was deep in the page before him, beefy fingers
etching piffle — random nouns — into notebook paper.
I bent till we were breathing each other's breath,
and savored the wincing intimacy as his smirk
withered. I'd been terrified. Now I was rashly happy
as I closed my lips gently over his nose. My future?
Pfft! Even being betrayed as a pervert
meant shit. Holding his shoulder against his rising,
I snapped my canines. He bucked hard once, went limp,
and I spat his blood onto his un-tensed un-sentences.

After Teaching

Who it Daddy? Who it Daddy? Joanie sang
when Benita rumbled up the aisle, a bull of a girl
leaning forward, falling from step to step. *Who
it Daddy? Who it Daddy?* And on the third day,
I saw, inside the larger swelling of Benita's swell,
an ancient couple turn a corner in an ancient city
and, holding hands, rise into twilight. They never fall,
the old couples who rise elegantly into evening.
No one finds them lying in wheat fields or draped over oaks
like collapsed balloons. Romantics say they rise forever,
but I believe they ascend so slowly they starve
before they strangle in the thin air, and then dissolve
in heaven's nothing. When I quit teaching,
I moved to that ancient city, and I ghosted there
the autobiography of a great man, a fascist sympathizer,
yes, but nothing more than that, he said. He loved willows,
willows of all kinds, and while I was articulating that love
I drank his purple wine and slept on his lubricious sheets.
Saying I, I, I, I made a self for him, noble but flawed, briefly
disoriented by boyish idealism — as I, I, I worked inside the green
curtain of the willows my words for him taught me to love.

Under the Horse

She snapped the reins and shouted "Brandon!" Hooves
crashed inches from my ears, and rose and crashed again.
How graceful it looks from a distance, I thought, this prancing.
Is it graceful now? And the gleaming mahogany flank,
is it beautiful when I'm frightened flinchless, transfixed
by the dried gray and darker damp mud fused
to the fetlock? Rose. "Brandon!" And crashed. The woman
hauled briskly on the reins and peered down miles of thigh
toward me. The huge bottom of her soaring, vertiginous
boot hooked, heel down hard, into the stirrup. Her scarlet jacket
glowed over me. Her black cap and lunar face floated
away in the cool cumulus sky. Rose. "Brandon!" she snapped,
and the only one of us that required a name came to rest.

The Blind Woman's Orchid

Her white cane's pink tip skittered over concrete as she approached,
blue eyes quivering in lavender sockets. Her pale fingers proprietary
on the arm I'd provided, we crossed the street I'd just crossed. "Coffee?"
I offered, and she almost understood. *The library's warm,* she said,
and clamped five dollars to my palm. "Oh, no . . . Please don't."
But she'd stepped into an office, an orchid on the windowsill —
alien, spectral, faint lavender streaked a pale Edenic blue.

I read Chekhov's *Selected Stories* all afternoon for free, and thought,
Selected Stories — why not selected witticisms, selected
late-night calls to selected exes — delete the drunk ones, save the sober?
The blind selected stranger granted me an afternoon of Chekhov
and a night nursing three beers till a drunk bought me a whiskey
and then another. I swayed with off-key strangers, belting
"Boil Them Cabbage Down, Boys," and under the wings
of the library's blue spruce, I woke, the onliest song I ever did sing
kazoo-ing in a dissociated skull. From work, I drive home now
past a blue neon martini, a triangle on a stalk, in it a jaunty olive.
In the olive, a pimiento winks a droll, red
come-hither, and, desiring desire, I remember, five nights a week,
an orchid's faint lavender corolla, cooling-toward-blue.

Abandoning the Play

They strode left and I slid out after
their disruption, and the woman's face,
I saw, was red — tears flicked
angrily away. The man, silent,
glowered, and then, heavily,
was gone. Her tears, now unhampered,
streamed down her face and long white neck.
Could I help? No, no, she was fine.
Coffee sometimes, talking sometimes
helps, and soon she was talking,
happy even, in the telling,
sipping coffee and then cognac,
my hands on hers, and then my mouth
on hers, and so on, till I was sitting
on the roof, home on slick slate, looking
through sagging phone wires and power lines.

I'd told her my mother had arisen
from her deathbed — I said "deathbed,"
I said "arisen" — to attend my wedding,
and I imagine Mother buried
in the hyacinth-blue suit she wore
that wasted, wintry day, smiling
when she had the energy to smile,
though — closed casket — I don't know.

For her story, she expected me
to tender passionate details
of course, and I offered truth so tired
that, for both of our nugatory stories,
it sounded like a lie.

A Handful of Keys

When I woke, a tailpipe thrummed inches from my face,
and it inquired, Sir, are you hurt? Solicitous automobile,
I thought till I saw my own owlish face regarding me from the black
sunglasses of a black state trooper who asked
if I'd been drinking. No, I don't think so, I answered, and thus
I walked an imagined tightrope and, with my head tilted to the stars,
I located my nose with first my left and then my right
index finger. This isn't a good place for dreaming,
said the sunglasses. Go home, they ordered. The cruiser
hurled itself into the paired lights rippling toward
me and away — lives reverberating feet from my feet, and judging
from the clutch of keys I held, I'd been one of them.
Sweet, I thought, looking at a Cadillac, pearl metallic
over gray leather. But where was home? The accelerator answered,
explaining for thirty miles, fifty, and then four hundred,
home was polished velocity and unembarrassed mass. Then
a red truck banged the Buick behind me and it, skewing,
bucked forward. I pushed my head hard into the headrest.
When's it coming? When's it coming? And it didn't. In the mirror,
the Buick, sideways, slashed into the median, ripping dry grass,
spraying brown gouts of it, and tumbled. *Yes, yes, yes!*
Lit with the rising sun, the black road opened before me.
Today the dream was my dream and I sang *yes!* —
a *yes* wrenched from another dreamer's *no*.

Blowfly

Half awake, I was imagining
a friend's young lover, her ash blonde hair, the smooth
taut skin of twenty. I imagined her
short legs and dimpled knees.
                              The door scraped open,
but eyes closed, I saw nothing. The mattress sagged.
She laid her head on my chest, and murmured love
against my throat, almost humming, approaching song,
so palpable I could hold her only chastely,
if this was chaste. I couldn't move my hand
even to caress her freckled shoulder.
So this is how imagination works, I thought,
sadly. And when at last she spoke,
she spoke with the amused voice of my wife,
my wife who was at work but also here,
pleased at the confusion she was causing.
This is a lesson about flesh, isn't it?
I asked. *Blowfly*, she whispered on my throat
as we made tense, pensive love. *Blowfly, blowfly*.

Outside the Inn

On the way out, I gripped his arm, squeezed, let go.
He was talking to another black suit
— we were all black suits for the funeral —
and his bicep shifted in my grip,
lax. (Had he been ill?) We smiled, nodded.
That was all, and, for old friends,
sufficient. Outside the inn, peonies, those
great nodding heads, unstable bobbers, climbed
the wall and spilt onto the roof, storming the inn.

"I didn't know peonies could do that," I said,
and my wife, marveling with me — red, pink,
and white petals stippling the bricks on which we stood —
replied, "They can't."
                              We parted the dark dull leaves,
and considered, in the shadows,
a hidden trellis, hung with green pots on green
hooks, and hundreds of neatly twisted green wires.

The inn opened behind us. Murmuring "We must, soon . . ."
"Yes, must," and reluctant to be seen
seeing, we stepped away from the green wall,
the impossible possible once more and beauty, in perspective,
beautiful. All afternoon and into evening,
I considered my house, car, wife, mirror —
close then distant, distant then close. All afternoon
and into evening, I placed myself before them, grieving.

Among Verbena

Among verbena at the yard's margin,
the verbena coming off bloom and the maples
into first leaf, the verbena's vertiginous perfume
overfilled the night's new warmth, and you,
with startled desire, knew it as mine —
verdant, fragrant, converging on a wavering Eden,
silver under the beams of a low moon
and promising more: blue lobelia
and unfurling herbage, none of which you knew
but knew I knew, as though I were your Virgil,
waving from the far verge of paradise
in a prospect of purple foxglove. Old friend,
I loved you for your envy. Through you, I too
saw beyond ivy's nearly irresistible invasion.
I was impervious to shabby grass overlapped with vinca.
The nugatory return from the babied,
barely surviving redbud did not perturb me; neither
did the morning glory that last year wove through wisteria
and arbor vitae, overshadowing them,
nor the moth larvae likely savoring my spirea,
and for a moment, I, observing your vision,
envied myself.

Came Back

When my mother came back,
— can I say it that way — *came back?* —
she flitted witlessly — kitchen,
living room, never settling,
like a child or a fly. Mom!
I called. Mom! Her eyes
flashed by me without lighting,
but she hesitated, and with
a kitchen knife, I slashed
my thumb. Blood, and she ran to me.
Blood, and she called my name.
What do you want? Say it!
I ordered, holding my hand
behind my back like a gift
for a child, for an adult a bribe.
She wanted blood. Blood
and her slippers. Funny. I'd
have guessed blood, cigarettes,
and a story to make her laugh.
She drank at my white hand
till I grew faint, then she drifted off.
For that minute, that moment, that
passage of time, I was
not childless, or a man.

The Circus

Yes, the girl sneezing pink froth and the woman fisting her eyes
each time another oldie crackles from the ceiling
look worse than I do. See them. And find, please, a dentist
for the man clutching two molars in a bloody paper towel.
And a CPA or lawyer — summon one for the man
squeezing the folder of gray paper to his chest and squeaking
grievously. But I have an *appointment*. I arrived two hours ago,
on time, a little early in fact, and someone must help me find
the Ferris wheel I hear looping in my attic and the Tilt-A-Whirl
lopsidedly unfolding and refolding in the basement.
Through the walls, I hear the *oompah-pah*ing of a carousel,
and in dark windows and the gleaming façades of black appliances
I glimpse ascending and descending carved horses, real tigers,
elephants, and waltzing poodles. Whitewashed clowns ghost across
a TV humbling itself before beer, soap, laundry, and my armpits, muffling
the human cannonball's applause and the dumbfounded wow
when orange torches enter a human face and emerge unquenched.
The circus is not my fault or responsibility. Someone
must *write that down*. Someone must sell me a ticket.

Cicada

Oracle of our mortal summers,
you rise, the encore of a ghost,
again and again from the earth, black here,
pale departed, prophesying,
through music, your return. Poets love you.
Apollo bestowed on you the high
Arcadian aria, a cadence
cascading from the self-shadowing leaves,
where, for your only food, you sip
the cool unfallen dew. Age
does not grind you like rancid grist
beneath its granite. Black among us,
pale departed, you have eluded mourning.
Your flesh bloodless, you do not suffer.
You are a song above our heads
in our hot corporeal evenings
until, from you, the darkness empties.

The Names of the Lost

The nights burned all night long that Freedom Summer —
ninety-four at midnight, eighty at dawn. Late June,
a high-speed chase. Goodman, Chaney, Schwerner

rammed off the road and hustled from their car.
Wayne Roberts asked, "Are you that nigger-lover?"
The nights burned all night long that Freedom Summer.

"I know exactly how you're feeling, sir,"
said Schwerner. Roberts shot him in the heart.
They shot them all: Goodman, Chaney, Schwerner.

"You didn't leave me nothing but a nigger,"
Jim Jordan griped. "But at least I killed me one."
The nights burned all night long that Freedom Summer.

Ray Killen prayed a funeral prayer. The preacher
beseeched God's mercy on these communists,
these agitators — Goodman, Chaney, Schwerner —

before they buried them, using a bulldozer.
The murderers, old men now, still walk the town.
The nights burned all night long that Freedom Summer.
Ask Andrew Goodman, James Chaney, Michael Schwerner.

Courtesy

I feel so bad for you, my friend,
your sufferings unsettle
my faith in meaning, I meant to say.
I hadn't meant to nettle

when, sad and blundering, I said,
"I know just how you feel,"
and got it slammed back: *"No
you don't. You couldn't."* "Fool!"

I didn't snap back even then.
Even then I didn't sigh,
"You're not the only heartsick boy
who's watched his mother die."

"I meant . . . I didn't mean . . . ," I stuttered.
It's not pain's magnitude
or the meanings we invent for it
we love — they are too crude —

but exclusivity. It's ours,
this pain, and thus unique.
Sure, other fools failed math, were snubbed
by the least exclusive clique,

and watched their mothers die in bright
cold antiseptic beds
with plastic tubes and coils of wire
exiting their heads.

Because they didn't love or hate
the same books, see the same
gray movies that we saw, adored,
and can no longer name,

they can't know us. They didn't sleep
with the same lovers seething
beside them. They can't hurt as we hurt
when we watched Mother's breathing

stall and go airless. Mom dies. You lose
a winning Lotto ticket.
A Peterbilt pancakes your cat.
Your house flares like a rocket.

All griefs, yet I would rank them, top
to bottom: dead mom, burnt house,
lost ticket, flat domestic shorthair.
Oh, there's a way, *of course,*

grief's grief. In the first moments, house,
Mom, ticket, Simon are all
the same — all lost in the paralyzed
identical sick pall

of loss, and when some stuttering,
well-meaning boy or girl
declares, "I know just how you feel,"
we don't disguise our snarl

and say, "I know you do," although
he may, that boy, have knelt
beside his brother by the lake,
and under his lips felt

his brother's pale blue flesh release
one last liquescent hiccup.
And at the register that girl
may have been ringing up

a forty and a pack of smokes
when a bullet blew apart
her boss's head and slapped his blood
across her blouse, like art,

like Pollock, she thinks. But we, still grieving,
know she can never know
how Simon purred into our ears
his gentle tremolo.

That boy and girl will see our grief
and offer theirs in kindness
and we'll reach out, in kindness too,
and introduce our blindness.

"You don't. You couldn't. No one could,"
we snarl at them, returning
the darkening wisdom of dark grief's
necessary spurning.

The Afterimage of a Ghost

Waking, I saw beyond my feet
a creature formed of light
step through the wall as if it were
a waterfall. His bright

face darkened but I was afraid
to pity him. This ghost
might be the only one I'd meet.
I sought its eye and almost,

almost spoke, before I turned away
faint-hearted. But I held
the snapshot memory of what I'd seen:
a bright face dark and cold

around stark cheekbones, hooded eyes,
tight disappointed mouth.
I studied that solipsistic oval,
a face swept into myth

against its will. By what? Lost love?
A plundered grave? A murder?
I studied memory until I saw
his pale eyes' strange disorder.

He'd strained to see the room, the walls,
the sleeper. But his stare
saw nothing I saw. Though he breathed,
he didn't breathe the air

that I inhaled, and though alive
— and so alive he pulsed —
he couldn't find me or the room
through which, staring, he passed

sightless. Again, I almost spoke
to help him help me learn
how I might surface in his eyes
from which I'd had to turn,

but when I turned again to look,
to look and maybe speak,
he was fading back into the wall's
alluring hide-and-seek

with everything I'd known of walls,
as bricks, not waterfalls,
though the cavern past the falls,
if it exists, enthralls.

The Bluebird, Singing, Leaps into the Sky

A dove erupts from brush. The hunter
swings, fires. In the glare,
a bluebird sweeping past the dove
crumples in midair,

while the dove beats on, undeviating.
"What the hell is wrong with you?"
his son grumbles. "An easy kill!"
His father tells him the blue

bird's magic blood splashed on the dove.
In the brief sinking glide
between the beating of its wings
the dove died and un-died,

and, not knowing it had died, flew on.
The boy snickers. He doesn't
believe this crap. Who would? The father
shrugs, and, his voice urgent,

rousts *his* tired father from the truck.
They crash through Queen Anne's Lace
till the father finds the broken bird
and scrubs it on his face

like a bar of soap. He hands the bird
to the old man, who scours
with the feathered scrap, then tosses it
into the weedy flowers,

sumac, and honeysuckle. The boy,
the forgotten boy, stares
at the raw clump while both men laugh
about aches and gray hairs.

"Do you feel younger?" "Not yet. Do you?"
A scream. They turn. The bluebird,
singing, leaps into the sky,
and from the sumac, bewildered,

running with outstretched bloodstained arms,
eyes shy and nearly wild,
there staggers toward them helplessly
the blue unborning child.

Epithalamium

Friends, we stood in church for you
as you knelt before the priest,
your faces glowing. Ours glowed too,
and our love for you increased

as we glanced at one another, and thought,
"It isn't going to last."
He's strayed before and she'll take comfort
as it's offered. She has in the past.

That's how you met. Did you wed in haste?
Or did you court too long
and settle into all-but-marriage?
Not right somehow. Not wrong.

"Careful," we thought approvingly
and then, "Too careful." But now
you're married, and we pray you won't
respect your wedding vow

for fear, the kids, or obligation
to prayers you would unpray,
as we have done — but from a choice
you choose again each day

with joy, each breath an affirmation,
as we have also done,
a few of us, after rage, raw sorrow,
change, and slow reunion.

American Rendering

We massacred Fort Mims, two hundred
and forty-seven souls,
if you count, as some did even then,
blacks, Indians, and mestizos,

all scalped, some tortured, *"and the females*
of every age were butchered
in a manner neither decency
nor seemliness of word

permit me to describe." The last
survivors huddled in
a stronghouse, begging, as they burned
to curled and dirty crackling —

burned by us, the Red Stick Creeks
of Alabama, just
recompense for those of us
they'd slaughtered. We rejoiced

almost a month, and an answer
fell on Tallusahatchee,
where we, now as a company
of whites from Tennessee,

ambushed a Creek encampment. Maybe
they were even Red Stick Creeks.
"We shot them like dogs," said Davy Crockett.
They fled to a hut. Groans. Shrieks.

We torched it. An Indian boy — twelve,
or thereabouts, his knees
shattered by gunfire — clawed at the dirt
in his last agonies.

"He lay so near the burning house
his grease stewed out of him,"
wrote Davy Crockett. We were famished,
three months from food and home,

and living on parched corn. We dug up
their hidden food — potatoes
buried beneath the gutted hut,
roasted in the inferno.

"Need forced us to the gray potatoes,
though I had rather not.
Oil had seeped down on them. They looked
like they'd been stewed with fat."

Gray potatoes, grease hardening.
We gorged on food they'd saved,
though all of us would rather not.
At the Alamo, we heaved

in his turn, Crockett on the pyre:
a layer of dry wood,
a layer of Texans. Mesquite, dead Texans.
The drunk priest said a word,

we lit the fire, and in just minutes
a scorched theriaca
haloed the flames, the grease by which
we render America.

Lightning Strike in Paradise

Jesus-the-wind combs Jesus-the-rye and shakes
the limbs of Jesus-the-scrub-pine-and-alder,
while a tractor, disking the rye, churns into the sunset
red clouds of Jesus. Jesus-the-bank-of-young-ferns
fringes Jesus-the-sluggish-and-rocky-stream
rich with tadpoles, crayfish, and almost invisible minnows,
all Jesus Himself. Jesus-the-green-worm inches up air.
He humps His body, pulls His end to His middle, and pushes
upward to where he started, climbing His own fine thread
until a gust of Jesus snaps the silk and sends Him flying.
Jesus-the-lightning explodes an oak. Jesus-the-thunder reverberates
through green leaves, the Jesus leaves, silencing
the Jesus-chitter of squirrels, wrens, and cicadas,
and in the distance the tractor never stops grinding
rye into the earth, preparing it for seed, as the unfixed
scent of sundered oxygen settles over heaven.

From

SAINTS AND STRANGERS
(1985)

The Persistence of Nature in Our Lives

You find them in the darker woods
occasionally — those swollen lumps
of fungus, twisted, moist, and yellow —
but when they show up on the lawn
it's like they've tracked me home. In spring
the persistence of nature in our lives
rises from below, drifts from above.
The pollen settles on my skin
and waits for me to bloom, trying
to work green magic on my flesh.
They're indiscriminate, these firs.
They'll mate with anything. A great
green-yellow cloud of pollen sifts
across the house. The waste of it
leaves nothing out — not even men.
The pollen doesn't care I'm not
a tree. The golden storm descends.
Wind lifts it from the branches, lofts
it in descending arches of need
and search, a grainy yellow haze
that settles over everything
as if it's all the same. I love
the utter waste of pollen, a scum
of it on every pond and puddle.
It rides the ripples and, when they dry,
remains, a line of yellow dust
zigzagging in the shape of waves.
One night, perhaps a little drunk,
I stretched out on the porch, watching

the Milky Way. At dawn I woke
to find a man-shape on the hard
wood floor, outlined in pollen — a sharp
spread-eagle figure drawn there like
the body at a murder scene.
Except for that spot, the whole damn house
glittered, green-gold. I wandered out
across the lawn, my bare feet damp
with dew, the wet ground soft, forgiving,
beneath my step. I understood
I am, as much as anyone,
the golden beast who staggers home,
in June, beneath the yearning trees.

The Choice the Driver Makes

Their headlights slash across my face and chest
and then the cars surge past, tires sizzling
in thin drizzle. I don't interest them
as I trudge through the tall wet grass beside
the road. I give them lots of room. It's late.
The drunks are out. And in work pants and dark shirt,
both drenched with rain, I am invisible
until the harsh lights choose me out of night
then blast into the further dark and drop me back
into darkness and give me back my sight.
Two lights veer off the road and aim at me.
For a long moment I stand judging them
almost convinced they'll swerve, then I leap
full-length into wet grass, wholeheartedly,
and cannot tell what choice the driver makes.

Something Wakes Me Up

Something wakes me up. I sit and listen.
A soggy rasp. A pause. Another rasp.
Someone is sawing. Not wood: it's too soft for wood.
There are two of them. They're trying to be quiet,
whispering but loudly. I part the blinds and look.
They've got it strung up from the swing set,
tongue bulging out, eyes huge with gravity.
They rinse her abdomen with a garden hose,
the water's hard stream ringing in the carcass.
Disturbed, I lie back down and close my eyes.
But once I know what's going on outside
each noise explains itself. I've done this before:
sat and listened to men do what I've imagined,
and not known how to stop them or turn them in.
The rasp returns — a higher pitch. They're sawing off
the hooves. And worst of all: long shearing rips
as they tear the skin from the tendons and yellow fat.
Then sawing again. Long sinking strokes: the head.
With hammer and chisel they split her down the spine
and toss the doe meat in their pickup beds.
It's quiet. The muscles of my neck relax.
And I get up and write it all to you
as a stronger man might simply ask forgiveness.

My Father's House

From a second-story window in my father's house
I see a steeple sway in the evening breeze.
The congregation's moved to a new brick church,
leaving the sagging steeple to the winds and wasps,
and to my father and the other folks
who've come to a random stop beside a church
that cannot mourn them: during the Great War
its bell went the way of many bells
when it was melted for its dollop of metal.
In the growing dark, the window turns
half mirror, a collage of in and out:
my face, the graves, the unhaunted church.
If this were a hundred, or even eighty, years ago
I could hear above the house the bluish peal
of thin bells breaking high on the night.

Late Spring in the Nuclear Age

for Clare Rossini

The fish hit water nymphs, breaking surface.
I hear the splash but when I turn to look
it's gone, the troubled water smoothing itself
back into blue glass. But sometimes I see it,
a bass wrench in midair as it pierces
the membrane of our world. How graceless it is,
the absolute half-second of its flight.

It's hard to say what's different.
It's not the bass. It's not that
I've seen two butterflies poised on one leaf,
their moist wings drying with slow rhythmic flaps.
The leaf quavered beneath their double weight.
Nor that above me on the hill I hear
a small boy hunting in the cemetery.
A hummingbird dissolves in the shotgun blast.
In water oaks the sparrows pause, don't sing,
then one by one their voices catch, unfurl,
as if they had forgotten what they heard.
But that is nothing new. We're used to death —
if not resigned. I stretch here on damp grass,
a paste of seeds and dew smeared on my boots,
trying to move the world into my mind
so I'll have it when summer settles in,
when it's too hot for blossom-set or talk
and nothing moves. This is what's different:
my prayer there'll be a summer to survive,
that our deaths will not be the last.

Magnolias

Alabama: the first, a girl child.
The rocking chair is cold, the porch colder,
but I could sit here for a year,
thinking of my child, her dwindling.

The magnolias too are windswept
graveward. Neither live oak nor reed
resists the weather's breath,
but each lets go its green, its living part.

Spring, when it comes, is at first wet,
becoming lush, giving way
to the darkgreen darkness
where magnolia leaves hover like wings,
inches off the receding earth.

Then the blooms on the tree will open.
They are so clearly flesh of
our flesh. Without the prolonging bone,
so clearly transitory.

When touched — and I touch them —
the blossoms smudge,
the flesh dying beneath my acid hands,
turning brown in the shape of fingertips.

Awaiting Winter Visitors:
Jonathan Edwards, 1749

When thunder fell in Tinsley's pasture
we recognized a sign from heaven.
From that day on we have rejoyced
that God has not forsaken us:
a blast upon the wavering wheat
is God's lean son walking ghost-
colored through our bodies, saying,
Yours is a famine of the soul.

On my advice the congregation met
six nights a week to pray and sing,
to burn the bushel off our flame.
Beneath the tired December sky
we looked for a descending light
to radiate from New England shores
to the almost mythic cusp of Asia.

Instead, the signs would not form
a prophecy. Attendance fell;
the fervor would not hold its bloom.
In March, hens in the cemetery
pecked up the younger Perkins boy,
who died of pox the winter past.
And yesterday the family cat

ate a poison spider, sickened, died.
I shall miss Joshua. Asleep on my lap
while I composed sermons, he'd purr

like a bit of Satan almost controlled.
At home Sarah's held to the hard faith.
We supped on vegetables and bones,
but mostly bones, those old friends

returning from other, more fleshy stews.
It built, it build to no climax
then passed to spring — with dandelions
and little purple weeds: the white
fields laced with merciless speedwell.
I shall retire and read St. Paul,
who called the human corpse a seed.

Madonna of the Pomegranate

after Botticelli

They crowd the blue triangle of the Madonna —
these adolescents who are also angels,
eyes staring everywhere but straight ahead,
absorbed in the changeless commerce of their world.
They're much like us. Some curiosities.
The wings that curve upward from their backs
are such unwieldy limbs — pure ornament —
you'd know that Botticelli made them up
even if you believed in messengers
with human wings. Where are the muscles
to lift an eighty-pound schoolgirl in the air?
And even if the wings are miracles
how do they get their tunics over them?
But wings aside, the angels look like kids.
One gossips, one has hard, suspicious eyes,
and several wear the slightly stupid look
most children wear when contemplating babies.
Madonna doesn't notice them. She's vague,
thin-faced, eyes drifting downward to the left,
a virgin holding her first child, cradling
him on the tips of her long, fragile fingers
as if she isn't sure where he came from —
so beautiful he almost isn't flesh.
Thus only Christ, unwavering, looks at us,
his left hand resting on a pomegranate
that splashes ruby light into the air,
his right hand raised in blessing or a wave
as he forgives us for not being art
or says goodbye since he will live forever.

Returning Home to Babylon

The eunuch who loves Daniel — Ashpenaz —
is not alone. It helps to think of him,
the loss he curls around to sleep, and how,
each night, he ushers to the king's bedchamber
a different woman. He watches. He decides
it's like entering a mirror, himself, a thing.
He knows how *other* Daniel is. He has
no choice, and if he did he'd take the whole
surplus of lust that might, perhaps, drive him
to slip alone into the prophet's cell.
He'd press his cheek against the other's cheek
and breathe the flesh-warm air beside his face.
Perhaps he'd simply shake the man awake
and whisper, *I love you.* He might go further.
He doesn't know. But love is even more dangerous
than lust or force. It can lead you to do
nothing. Lead you to abstinence and silence.
Lead you to Ashpenaz, a man I envy
because I envy the driven. They've ceased
to agonize on what or why — just how.
But passion stops at nothing. There are women
whom I, in awe of waking, have watched sleep
and I have ached to hold my face
down next to theirs, almost touching, and breathe
their breath, which will be sour with sleep,
raw in the heat of dreams. But if I breathed it,
I'd want to kiss their parted, sleeping lips
and if they wakened to the kiss I'd want
to love them as I loved another woman.

Sloping above me like the ceiling of
an attic room, sweat streaming from her face
and onto mine, she laughed, and as she came
she whispered in my ear, *Goddamn you! God-
damn you! Goddamn you!* And though I didn't want
the love to understand, I understood.
We grew so strange in love and understanding
we couldn't risk talking. But Ashpenaz
risks his life to bring Daniel water, bread,
fresh plums, and, once, a spider trapped in amber.
Even these are nothing. Trash. As gifts, he brings
his dreams. And it is terrible to see
the prophet fall on them each day, savage
as a street dog during siege or famine.
And if the frightened eunuch will not talk
Daniel grabs him by the hand and cries,
You dreamed this! This is what you dreamed!
And then he tells the eunuch what it means,
and in detail.

      My love, we were more careful.
Perhaps too careful. I no longer know.
Each night sleep lifted us up off the sheets
where we lay side by fragile, sleeping side
lost separately in the same domain of fierce
outlandish couplings with other people —
mothers, strangers, men. We have a need
to learn, in there, the loves forbidden here.
But what we learn we may not want to know.

Returning home, still dazzled at the crossing,
we now and then forget we've left our dreams
whose outlaw grace allows us anything,

and we are slightly strange to one another,
formal and wary, not sure what we might do.
The eunuch knows what he is doing. After
long hours divulging dreams, he walks alone
into the cool air of the palace hall.
The vessels the slaves fill with water sway
above his head, cooling the rooms. In summer
they lift them down three times a day, then cart
them to the river, a dozen at a time.
Two hundred vessels. Clay. They break at least
one jug a day. They're beaten for their lack
of grace, their clumsiness. And they should be
because we must be careful in a world
that breaks so easily beneath our hands,
even for Ashpenaz — a careful man.
This eunuch from four thousand years ago
who may have never lived, this man I love,
walks home beneath the fragile, hanging jars,
heading toward sleep as some men head to work,
returning to his dreams as if he'd lost
something in there, where each half of the mind
pitches itself against the other half
with so much rage it is both bite and kiss,
devour and complete. Toward dawn they tear
themselves apart — awed, dumb, and unappeased —
and Ashpenaz throws on his robe and runs
to tell it all to Daniel, who already knows.

Saints and Strangers

1. AT THE PIANO

One night two hunters, drunk, came in the tent.
They fired their guns and stood there stupidly
as Daddy left the pulpit, stalked toward them,
and slapped them each across the mouth. He split
one's upper lip.

          They beat him like a dog.
They propped their guns against the center pole,
rolled up their sleeves as Daddy stood and preached
about the desecration of God's house.
They punched him down, took turns kicking his ribs,
while thirty old women and sixteen men
sat slack-jawed in their folding chairs and watched.
Just twelve, not knowing what to do, I launched
into "Amazing Grace" — the only hymn
I knew by heart — and everybody sang.
We sang until the hunters grew ashamed
— or maybe tired — and left, taking their guns,
their faces red and gleaming from the work.

They got three years' suspended sentence each
and Daddy got another tale of how
Christians are saints and strangers in the world.
He said I, and God's music, saved his life.
But I don't know. I couldn't make a guess.
Can you imagine what it means to be
just barely twelve, a Christian and a girl,
and see your father beaten to a pulp?

Neither can I, God knows, and I was there
in the hot tent, beneath the mildewed cloth,
breathing the August, Alabama air,
and I don't know what happened there, to me.
I told this to my second husband, Jim.
We were just dating then. I cried a lot.
He said, *Hush, dear, at least your father got*
a chance to turn all four of his cheeks.
I laughed. I knew, right then, I was in love.
But still I see that image of my father,
his weight humped on his shoulders as he tried
to stand, and I kept plunging through the song
so I could watch my hands and not his face,
which was rouged crimson with red clay and blood.

2. EVE'S SIN

Some summer nights when we were on the road
we slept in sleeping bags inside the tent —
money. I'd listen to mosquitoes sing,
how they go oddly silent as they strike.
If I were bored enough I'd let them land
and fill themselves with blood. Then I'd decide
if I would let them go or slap them dead,
knowing I'd wake to find the purple flecks
smudged randomly across my neck and arms.

As I removed my dress to go to sleep,
I saw my underpants were dark with blood.
There wasn't any pain but I was scared.
I called, *Daddy?* He said, *Hush, Marie.*
I said, *I'm bleeding, Daddy.* He was strange,
yet happy too. He held my hands and said,
*This happens to all little girls. I should
have mentioned it. You'll bleed like this each month —
about five days. It's* . . . He paused and thought,
and that long pause scared me so bad I cried
until I vomited. It sounded so
illogical. I was convinced that I
was dying. It took me years to figure out
that he'd almost explained the sin of Eve
which every woman suffers for. But that
was years later. He rocked me like a child.
He whispered, *Hush now, baby. Hush yourself,*
kissed my drenched cheeks, and zipped me in the bag,
an undershirt clenched hard between my thighs.

3. WHERE THE RIVER JORDAN ENDS

She put two flowered hair clasps in my hair.
They held. I was amazed. Though Daddy thought
I should be wearing ribbons on my head
he couldn't make them stay. One Christmas Day
he saved the ribbons left from opening gifts
and looped them through my curls. We went to church,
where Aunt Bess snickered, picked them from my hair
and off my neck. She told Daddy, *Jerome,*
she's festooned like a nigger Christmas tree.
But Mrs. Shores knew everything! She smiled
and smoothed my hair around the flowered clasps.
Her husband had invited Daddy down
to preach a week's revival at his church,
and she, since I was almost thirteen, let me
drink coffee when the men were off at work.

Their son took me and Sis into the church.
We ran around the aisles till we got tired,
then shucked our shoes and socks, sat on the rail,
and dangled feet into the River Jordan —
a painting on the wall that seemed to flow
into the baptistery. We splashed around,
got wet, then stripped down to our birthday suits,
and leapt into the font. We went berserk.
We were cannonballing off the rail
when Daddy threw the double doors apart.
We jumped into the font and held our breath.
When I came up, Daddy was standing there,
waiting. I flinched. Instead he touched my cheek:
Put on your clothes, Elizabeth Marie.
And then I saw the tears. I cried all day.

That night as I sat staring at the wall
behind my father, where the Jordan ends,
I heard God's voice and went to be immersed,
trembling and happy in a paper robe,
and Daddy hugged my body to his chest.
I left a wet, dark shadow on his suit.
I wanted to be saved again. Again.

4. LOOSE CHANGE

We'd sip our water and wait till supper came,
then he'd return thanks. It was never quick
or done by rote. It was heartfelt — and loud —
while everybody in the truck stop watched.
They tried to do it secretly, the way
you look at cripples, retards, droolers, freaks.
I'd raise my head and watch them watching us,
and once, seeing my head unbowed, he said,
Elizabeth Marie, please close your eyes.
He says that we are strangers here on earth
and it is true I've never felt at home.
In Denver, once, a man asked me the way
to Mile High Stadium, and though I'd been
in town almost two years and had a job
I said, *I am a stranger here myself,*
amazed at what was coming from my lips.
Are you okay? he asked. How could I say
that I'd been talking bad theology?
But it was worse for Daddy, I suspect.
At least I watched the world and tried to make
accommodation. Since he wouldn't tip
I lifted loose change from the offering plate
to slip onto the table as we left.
Staring right at the waitress, I would think,
Take this, you slut, I've stolen it for you.

5. THE SOUTHERN CRESCENT WAS ON TIME

I played piano while my daddy knelt,
unlaced their shoes, and washed the clean pink feet
they'd washed before they'd come to have them washed.
He never just slopped water on the feet
like some men do. Instead he lifted each foot,
working the soapy rag between their toes
with such relentless tenderness the boys
would giggle, girls would blush, and women sigh.
And though the feet looked clean to begin with,
when he was done the water was as black
as crankcase oil.
                                And then he'd preach, preach hard.
Black suit, black tie, white shirt gone limp with heat,
he'd slap the pulpit and a spray of sweat
would fly into the air. He'd wipe his brow,
letting the silence work into the crowd,
and then start low, or with — almost — a shout.
I never could guess which. His face would gleam
with sweat. It was as if he were, each night,
baptizing himself from the inside out.

As you drive home tonight, he'd say, *a truck,*
a diesel truck,
                    might cross into your lane
and you would die apart from God,
                                        unsaved.
One night a pair of twins sat in this tent
and each one heard God speaking to his heart.
One twin came forward to be saved,
                                        and one
stayed in his seat,

resisted God's free grace.
He needed time to think — or so he thought —
but you can't know when God will take you back.
The earth is not our home. We're passing through.
That night

        as they drove to the Dairy Queen
their brand-new car stalled on the railroad track.
That night

        the Southern Crescent was on time.
One went to heaven with his loving God,
and we know where the other went,

                don't we?
The place where you are bathed in clinging fire
and it will last forever,

           burning, burning,
and you will beg to die.

           But you can't die
because, poor fool,

        you are already dead.

He'd wipe his forehead with a handkerchief.

If you should die tonight where will your soul
reside for all eternity?

           In fire?
Or will you sit, in grace, at God's right hand?
Come up for God's free cleansing love.

               Come up.
Let Jesus take your sins away.

               Come up.

They'd come and Daddy dunked them on the spot
so they could face the family car in peace.

Waiting for them as they lurched down the aisle,
he stood, head bowed, arms raised above his head,
and I would play until his hands came down
and touched his belt. And once I played
twenty-two verses of "Just As I Am"
while Daddy stood there stubbornly, arms raised,
waiting for God to move their hardened hearts.
I prayed that someone would be saved. My sweat
dripped on my hands. My fingers cramped
and skittered on the keys, then I passed out.

                When I came to,
the crowd was gone and Daddy's coat was tucked
beneath my head. He rubbed my arms, rolling
the limp flesh back and forth between his hands.
His eyes were focused past the empty chairs
and out the door. His lips moved silently
so I could tell he was praying for me.
But what, I didn't ask or want to know.

6. A KISS IN CHURCH

I had to giggle at the way he sang
"Amazing Grace" like Donald Duck. And once,
while everybody's head was bowed, he kissed
me on the mouth. But Daddy saw the kiss
and later, after church, he yelled at me.
I was too big — too old — for him to slap.
He wouldn't stop yelling. I wouldn't cry
or say that I'd done wrong. Next thing I knew
I was married. Though Daddy says I was,
I don't remember being asked. Bud was
a handsome boy. So Daddy could be right.
But for the longest time after I left
I kept this scene to jab into my heart:
Bud sitting, dirty, at the kitchen table,
his flannel sleeves rolled past his elbows.
He's giving me that hangdog look of his
I stand in the doorway, adamant,
my second baby straddling my hip.
How can he be so meaningless, who once
was everything. And what am I to him?
Nothing. I hope nothing. Nothing at all.

7. GLOSSOLALIA

There was one sagging bed, all his. We slept
on quilts — a pallet in the living room —
and listened to his shallow, rasping breaths
assert themselves against the growl and suck
of diesels on the interstate. They made
the whole house shake. While Sis was off at work
I wiped dried Maalox from his lips, fed him,
and prayed as best I could. And I'd call home
and talk for hours to the girls and Jim
until I couldn't tell the phone calls from
the prayers. Daddy's speech returned to English
and we could understand, at last, the words,
which up till then had been a random, wild
intensity of esses. It sounded like
the tongues of fire, the glossolalia
that slithers off the otherworldly tongues
of people baptized in the Holy Ghost.
His demons suddenly were visible
and he'd been talking to them in a tongue
we couldn't understand. It frightened us.
It was like we were children once again
and there was Daddy once again endowed
with knowledge of a world we couldn't see.

When he walked off, the sheriff brought him back
and helped me tuck him in. Over iced tea,
he said that Daddy'd run through Kroger's, shouting
and pointing out the demons. One lady screamed
when Daddy shouted in her face, *My God!*
One's chewing on your ear! The sheriff thought
that was a hoot. He laughed and slapped his thigh.

At supper Sis got mad and screamed at me
for letting him stray off. I let it slide
and passed the meat. That night, rising to pee,
I found her curled up on Daddy's bed.
He was asleep and she was sleeping too,
her face unaging as she shed the world,
and she was shining: light trickled down her face,
her cheeks. It shone like streams of molten solder.
Silver would sound more beautiful and it
was beautiful. It took my breath away.
But I have never seen molten silver.
Or molten glass.
           I made my mind up then
she didn't have the strength to care for Daddy.
It was my turn. Before I left, we sold
the loaded truck, the folding chairs, the tent.
Almost nine hundred bucks. The root of evil.
Enough for her to let her sainthood go.
And if I wouldn't change a thing — not this,
not anything — is that a lack of faith?
Too much imagination? Not enough?

You teach a Baptist etiquette, she turns
Episcopalian. I did. It's calm.
And Daddy, who shudders when I take the host,
stays home and worships with the TV set.
He's scared to leave the house. Incontinence.
When he's wet himself, he lets us know
by standing grimly at our bedroom door
and reading from his Bible. We think about
a nursing home. If I put on Ray Charles
he huffs around the house and says, *Marie,*
that nigger jungle-thumping hurts my head.
But these are little things. In many ways
the stroke has helped. He's gentle with the girls.
For hours he'll ride them horsy on his knees.
Still, there are those damn demons. Mine are blue,
Jim's red. He whispers demons to the girls
and gets them so they don't know what to think
of us. Beth's asthma starts. I tell the girls,
You play pretend, don't you? Well, you can stop.
But Paw-paw can't. He always plays pretend.
They seem to understand. In some ways, though,
I think he's even purer now — a saint
of all his biases, almost beyond
the brute correction of our daily lives.
Strangeness is part of it. And rage and will.
There's something noble in that suffering
and something stupid too. I'm not a saint,
of course, but as a child I had a rage
I've lost to age, to sex, to understanding,
which takes the edge off everything. Perhaps
it's my metabolism cooling down.

Who knows? One glory of a family is
you'd never choose your kin and can't unchoose
your daddy's hazel eyes — no more than you
could unchoose your hand. You get to be,
in turn, someone you'd never choose to be.
When feeling strong, I'll ask him to give thanks.
If he goes on too long, I say amen
and pass whatever bowl is near at hand.
Jim carves the meat, the girls reach for their tea,
and Daddy takes the bowl and helps his plate.

From

AFTER THE LOST WAR
(1988)

Child on the Marsh

I worked the river's slick banks, grabbing
in mud holes underneath tree roots.
You'd think it would be dangerous,
but I never came up with a cooter
or cottonmouth hung on my fingertips.
Occasionally, though, I leapt upright,
my fingers hooked through the red gills
of a mudcat. And then I thrilled
the thrill my father felt when he
burst home from fishing, drunk, and yelled,
well before dawn, *"Wake up! Come here!"*
He tossed some fatwood on the fire
and flames raged, spat, and flickered. He held
a four-foot mudcat. *"I caught it!"*
he yelled. *"I caught this monster!"* At first,
dream-dazed, I thought it was something
he'd saved us from. By firelight, the fish
gleamed wickedly. But Father laughed
and hugged me hard, pressing my head
against his coat, which stank, and glittered
where dried scales caught the light. For breakfast,
he fried enormous chunks of fish,
the whole house glorious for days
with their rich stink. One scale stuck to my face,
and as we ate he blinked, until
he understood what made me glitter.
He laughed, reached over, flicked the star
off of my face. That's how I felt
— that wild — when I jerked struggling fish

out of the mud and held them up,
long muscles shuddering on my fingers.
Once, grabbing, I got lost. I traced
the river to the marsh, absorbed
with fishing, then absorbed with ants.
With a flat piece of bark, I'd scoop
red ants onto a black-ant hill
and watch. Then I would shovel black
ants on a red-ant hill to see
what difference that would make.
Not much. And I returned to grabbing,
then skimming stones. Before I knew it,
I'd worked my way from fresh water to salt,
and I was lost. Sawgrass waved, swayed,
and swung above my head. Pushed down,
it sprang back. Slashed at, it slashed back.
All I could see was sawgrass. Where was
the sea, where land? With every step,
the mud sucked at my feet with gasps
and sobs that came so close to speech
I sang in harmony with them.
My footprints filled with brine as I
walked on, still fascinated with
the sweat bees, hornets, burrow bees;
and, God forgive me, I was not afraid
of anything. Lost in sawgrass,
I knew for sure just *up* and *down*.
Almost enough. Since then, they are
the only things I've had much faith in.
Night fell. The slow moon rose from sawgrass.
Soon afterward I heard some cries
and answered them. So I was saved
from things I didn't want to be

saved from. Ma tested her green switch
— *zip! zip!* — then laid it on my thighs,
oh, maybe twice, before she fell,
in tears, across my neck. She sobbed
and combed my hair of cockleburs.
She laughed as she dabbed turpentine
onto my cuts. I flinched. She chuckled.
And even as a child, I heard,
inside her sobs and chuckling,
the lovely sucking sound of earth
that followed me, gasped, called my name
as I stomped through the mud, wrenched free,
and heard the earth's voice under me.

At Chancellorsville

The Battle of the Wilderness

He was an Indiana corporal
shot in the thigh when their line broke
in animal disarray. He'd crawled
into the shade and bled to death.
My uniform was shabby with
continuous wear, worn down to threads
by the inside friction of my flesh on cloth.
The armpit seams were rotted through
and almost half the buttons had dropped off.
My brother said I should remove
the Yank's clean shirt: "From now on, Sid,
he'll have no use for it." Imagining
the slack flesh shifting underneath
my hands, the other-person stink
of that man's shirt, so newly his,
I cursed Clifford from his eyeballs to
his feet. I'd never talked that way before
and didn't know I could. When we returned,
someone had beat me to the shirt.
So I had compromised my soul
for nothing I would want to use —
some knowledge I could do without.
Clifford, thank God, just laughed. It was good
stout wool, unmarked by blood.
By autumn, we wore so much blue
we could have passed for New York infantry.

On the Killing Floor

The cows moaned deep bass lows that rumbled in
their bellies as I toddled under them,
a child of four. I'd crawled beneath the fence
to feel the huge notes tremble on my flesh.
My short head scraping on their bellies, I walked

between tall legs, feet gumming in the mud
of the small pen outside the slaughterhouse.
I've marveled at how placidly they go
to death, as, later still, I marveled at
how cheerfully in war men march to death

and me in step with them. A penned-up herd
of horses might have spooked, and trampled me.
But cows are stupid meat. How large they were!
Great docile things that somehow frightened me
by size alone. What else about a cow

is there to frighten anyone, except
how well behaved they are in line to die?
If you stare most beasts in the eye — dogs, cats —
you see a fleck of light that might be called
a soul. In cow's thick, clouded, mud-colored eyes,

I've never seen a thing. Is that light why
we don't eat horses, dogs, or cats
unless we must? Horse isn't bad. But that
is all I know about forbidden flesh.
And which was I among those moaning cows?

They jostled slowly one against the other.
I grabbed a heifer's tail and followed her
onto the killing floor. I don't recall
the nine-pound hammer's soft report, the cow's
thud as she fell, the sudden twisting of

her tail, which I would not let go, my gasp
as a huge black man swung me by the waist
and said, "Don't rush. You'll get here soon enough."
He laughed and carried me beneath his arm
to Mama, who says she screamed and wept.

I don't remember any of these things.
But I'll remember till I die the way
she switched me with a green althea switch
I had to choose myself. *Swick, swick,* it said
across my butt. *Don't be so curious.*

Burial Detail

Between each layer of tattered, broken flesh
we spread, like frosting, a layer of lime,
and then we spread it extra thick on top
as though we were building a giant torte.
The lime has something to do with cholera
and helps, I think, the chemistry of decay
when slathered between the ranks of sour dead.
I know what we did; I'm not sure why.
The colonel had to ask us twice for volunteers;
the second time I went. I don't know why.
Even in August heat I cannot sleep
unless I have a sheet across my shoulders.
I guess we owe our species something.
We stacked the flaccid meat all afternoon,
and then night fell so black and absolute
it was as if the day had never been,
was something impossible we'd made up
to comfort ourselves in our long work.
And even in the pitch-black, pointless dark
we stacked the men and spread the lime
as we had done all day. Though not as neatly.

I didn't look; I didn't sift their pockets.
A lot of things got buried that shouldn't have been.
I tossed men unexamined into the trench.
But out of the corner of my eyes
I kept seeing faces I thought I knew.
At first they were the faces of anonymous men
I may have seen in camp or on the field.

Later, as I grew tired, exhausted, sick,
I saw they were my mother, father, kin
whom I had never seen but recognized
by features I knew in different combinations
on the shifting, similar faces of my cousins,
and even, once, a face that looked like mine.
But when I stopped to stare at them
I found the soft, unfocused eyes of strangers
and let them drop into the common grave.
Then, my knees gave. I dropped my shovel
and pitched, face first, into the half-filled trench.
I woke almost immediately, and stood
on someone's chest while tired hands pulled me out.
It's funny; standing there, I didn't feel
the mud-wet suck of death beneath my feet
as I had felt it often enough before
when we made forced marches through Virginia rain.
That is to say, the dead man's spongy chest
was firmer than the roads that led us —
and him — into the Wilderness.
For six or seven days I had to hear
a lot of stupid jokes about that faint:
folks are dying to get in, that sort of thing.
I wasn't the only one to faint.
You'd think I would have fainted for my father,
for some especially mutilated boy,
for Clifford or my mother. Not for myself.

In the hot inexhaustible work of the night
a good wind blowing from a distant storm
was heaven, more so because the bodies needed
to be wet, to ripen in moisture and lime,
to pitch and rock with tiny lives,

or whatever it takes to make them earth again.
Okay, I'm sorry for this, for getting worked up.
The thought that they might not decay
was enough to make my stomach heave.
Some men I've argued with seem to think
that they'll stay perfect, whole and sweet,
beneath the ground. It makes me shudder:
dead bodies in no way different from my own
except mine moves, and shudders in its moving.
I take great comfort in knowing I will rot
and that the chest I once stood on
is indistinguishable from other soil
and I will be indistinguishable from it.

But standing there, looking out of the grave,
eyes barely above the lip of the earth, I saw
the most beautiful thing I've ever seen:
dawn on the field after the Wilderness.
The bodies, in dawn light, were simply forms;
the landscape seemed abstract, unreal.
It didn't look like corpses, trees, or sky,
but shapes on shapes against a field of gray
and in the distance a source of doubtful light,
itself still gray and close to darkness.
There were a thousand shades of gray,
with colors — some blue perhaps and maybe green —
trying to assert themselves against that gray.
In short, it looked like nothing human.
But sun broke the horizon soon enough
and we could see exactly what we'd done.

After the Lost War

In Montgomery — August 1866

1.

A walk abroad our Sunday streets
is like a stroll thought lost Pompeii,
though our lives aren't so interesting
as theirs, at least as Bulwer-Lytton tells
of them in his book on the last days.
If you went on a Sunday walk with me,
you'd see that almost nothing moves.
The trees stand motionless, like statues,
and even when a breeze steals in,
the leaves flap once, then idly swing
in dull, half-hearted remonstrance
at the disturbance of their rest.
Our weekday streets are much like Sunday's
so business, as you might expect,
sets no one's heart to fluttering.
I don't believe a man in town
could be induced to go into
his neighbor's store and ask, "How's trade?"
He'd have to make amends
for such an insult all his life.
Even the bugs refuse to move
in all this seething heat. Alone
among insects, the bee — beloved
of Virgil for his industry —
is always busy, foraging
even into the midst of town

and seeking out the last coarse rose
or random violet. But then,
after the bees have ceased their toil,
our streets show no life save late in
the afternoon, when girls come out,
slowly, one by one, and shine and move,
as do the stars an hour later.

2.

I don't intend to quarrel with summer.
This is the first since sixty-one
I haven't dressed in butternut.
Yet even in this pastoral land
the green is mixed with battle cries
and phantom groans. A handsome spring
it was. But, my sweet God, to me
the flowers stank of sulfur and
their blooms were flecked with human blood.

At night I think much of the sea.

3.

Come fall I hope to travel north
with the manuscript of *Tiger-Lilies*,
on which I try to work at night,
while moths like dusty knuckles rap
the lighted glass. Before midnight,
when the sultry air is somewhat cooled,
the mockingbirds refuse to sing.
I wait for them. And out my window
the fireflies flicker slower than
I've ever seen those tiny lights.

Our world yawns in a witchery
of laziness. On us is cast
a spell, "an exposition of sleep"
as overtook Sweet Bully Bottom.
The proper term is *aestivation,*
a word that I'm enchanted with.

4.

I've heard they nearly always follow
the river's course — the flaring birds
that arch across the late-night sky
from time to time. I had no way
of guessing what they were: not stars —
though higher than the fireflies rise,
they fly too low for stars. I asked around
and found that drunken sailors set
meat scraps along the riverbanks
and with a crude trap made of rope
ensnare the buzzards they attract.

These birds, kept tied till after dark,
they douse with kerosene, set on fire,
then launch into the evening sky.
The burning makes them fly quite high;
the flying expedites the burning —
it progresses geometrically
until they fall, like burnt-out stars,
into the Alabama River.
One night, preoccupied with work,
I think I made a wish on one.

For them it must be hideous,
but from the ground it's beautiful —

in some odd way an easement of
the savage tedium of days.
But more than that: perhaps you know,
with the younger generation of the South
after the lost war, pretty much
the whole of life has been not dying.
And that is why, I think, for me
it is a comfort just to see
the deathbird fly so prettily.

Raven Days

These are what my father calls
our raven days. The phrase is new
to me. I'm not sure what it means.
If it means we're hungry, it's right.
If it means we live on carrion,
it's right. It's also true
that every time we raise a voice
to sing, we make a caw and screech,
a raucous keening for the dead,
of whom we have more than our share.
But the raven's an ambiguous bird.
He forebodes death, and yet he fed
Elijah in the wilderness
and doing so fed all of us.
He knows his way around a desert
and a corpse, and these are useful skills.

Reflections on Cold Harbor

It's after dawn the third of June
— ninth anniversary of Cold Harbor —
and I, who rose before the sun
to walk the darkness from the woods,

am sitting in a neighbor's field
and watching as the early sun
burns off the last dew from the corn.
From men I was in prison with

I heard that Grant's men looked like corn
advancing toward the reaper's blade,
on which they fell relentlessly. That June,

the fields were soaked with summer rain.
If they had actually been corn
we never would have harvested — not wet,
ripe corn. It spoils. As did those men.

Elijah Cobb said that as he fired
into the massive surging of their line
he started crying. Tears blurred his aim.
But he did not withhold his fire:

there were so many running men
that every shot hit something blue,
even a shot fired blind through tears.
He was embarrassed by those tears

and couldn't understand their cause.
And knowing Cobb, a man who once
staged cockroach races for the troops
then ate the winner live, neither can I.

So now I sit amid the corn
and think about the quantities
of fertilizer it requires
— much more than other plants —

and how it's pollinated not by bees
but the vagaries of the summer wind.
The dark sky brightens to deep-ocean blue,
a blue in which some poets have

been known to drown quite happily.
But that's a trick the language plays
with some help from my nervous system
and a human wish to flee the body.

Sometimes, like now, I have great need
to live outside of metaphor,
to know a dawn that's only dawn
and corn that's corn and nothing else.

Fishkill on the Chattahoochee

I pushed a dead fish down and held it under.
It wouldn't stay. When I removed my hand
the fish bobbed up, and as I grabbed for it
I stung my middle finger on its fin.
Up close, the fish were a nasty, stinking mess.
I started home but had to turn and look,
and from a distance the acre of dead fish
shimmered like enchanted cobblestones.
From a hill above the Chattahoochee's banks,
I saw the moonlit silver of the fish
catching the light like a length of shining road
that, in another world, had broken free
and drifted down to us with promises
that radiant stones would bear our weight
and the road would lead us to its world.
I forget sometimes the power of the moon.
The unfair beauty of reflected light
made me forget that yesterday the fish
did more than drift downstream atop the current.
But I will tell you this, and it frightens me:
from the hill, removed from individual deaths,
it was the most beautiful thing I've ever seen.
I watched the road and all its borrowed light
move slowly toward the sea — then walked back home,
with care, as though the road beneath my feet
were not as real or solid as I'd thought
despite a drop of blood that fell from my cut,
the blood just barely darker than the clay.

The Summer of the Drought

He wasn't right. We all knew that. His head
bulged oddly on the left above his eye
and he'd eat anything that he could cram
into his mouth. Once, at the creek, I saw
him catching polliwogs and slurping them
out of his palms. I made him stop, of course,
and walked him home, but later he sneaked back,
and Mary saw him down there eating clay.
Then, in the summer of the drought, the streams
dried up and he crawled underneath our house
to cool down in the dark. I'm guessing now.
He found a wasp nest, grabbed it from the brace,
and stuffed the boiling lump into his mouth.
At least that's what I figure must have happened.
He never talked again. And coming through
the floor beneath my feet, his scream was high
and thin, like flimsy metal being ground.
I was sitting at the table, drinking tea.
The air was heavy with the scent of sulfur
and lilac. I felt it vibrate through my feet.
The human whine of metal being ground.

Listen! The Flies

I went there early with a bamboo fan,
but every time I paused to greet a friend
the flies would settle back. I'd fan again.
They'd scatter out into the kitchen with

a lazy, slow, resentful tremolo.
It was August — the sort of weather that
makes flies affectionate of flesh
even when it's alive. And Gibson wasn't.

His coffin stretched across four straight-back chairs
set in the parlor. Though he was newly dead,
the flies, prescient, knew he belonged to them.
They find what's theirs: outside the surgeon's tent,

the three-foot hill of amputated limbs
shimmered with flies, as if the whole pile struggled
to pull itself together and walk off —
a beast entirely made of arms and legs.

In prison camp, the flies were fond of us.
I learned to praise the flies. By Gibson's corpse
the preacher had us rise to sing a lie:

"The Green Blade Riseth." I sang along. Although
I've walked the marsh and seen the green blade split
the dried-out clump, I've also been to war.
I know that everything that lives is pitched

from purity to putrefaction, back
and forth. But for the individual corpse
it's permanent. The green blade riseth, yes,
but Mrs. Gibson's Jeff is gone for good.

The Bible doesn't countenance these lies:
from ash to ash, it says, from dust to dust,
with fire and dirty water in between.
Or maybe they are passed to other dust

the way a lie that's passed from ear to ear
might turn into the truth along the way.
I've given this some thought. In winter, mist
rose from the piles as each lopped arm and leg

gave up its fraction of the soul. Last week
a fly got in my room and walked across
my face. The creeping tickle woke me up.
I slapped at it so hard I hurt myself.

Later I got him trapped behind the drapes
and made short work of him. But he'll be back — or one
so much alike it might as well be him.
That changing permanence is what I praise.

His Wife

My wife is not afraid of dirt.
She spends each morning gardening,
stooped over, watering, pulling weeds,
removing insects from her plants
and pinching them until they burst.
She won't grow marigolds or hollyhocks,
just onions, eggplants, peppers, peas —
things we can eat. And while she sweats
I'm working on my poetry and flute.
Then growing tired of all that art,
I've strolled out to the garden plot
and seen her pull a tomato from the vine
and bite into the unwashed fruit
like a soft, hot apple in her hand.
The juice streams down her dirty chin
and tiny seeds stick to her lips.
Her eye is clear, her body full of light,
and when, at night, I hold her close,
she smells of mint and lemon balm.

A Husband on the Marsh

I'm lost. Which is the point. That's why
I come here when I can and walk
the marsh. Well, not exactly lost.
Over scrub pines, I recognize
a cypress that's not too far from the road
back home. I know the marsh too well.
I can't get lost — unlike when I
was just a child. With longer legs,
I see above sawgrass. I know
the stars. I know which side of trees
moss dangles from. I always find
my way back home without much drama.
Or much fear. Even if I stare
into the sun, then close my eyes
and follow the two dots of fire
scored on the back of my eyelids
like stars, I can't get lost. I just
get my feet drenched from stumbling
into water, clothes scuffed from brushing
against trees, my face lashed with limbs,
hands slashed by sawgrass. But when I look
I know exactly where I am.
Or will: This run of rotting fence
connects to Parker's land. This smoke
wafts from a chimney whose fireplace
I've sat by and talked politics.

But I get lost in what it means —
the marsh. Mary just says, "Who cares?"

When I was young I had no doubt
the marsh — the world — was God's mind. We
were God's thoughts as we trampled through
the bog, fished, hunted deer, and tried
to keep our awe in check. Why try?
But then I started in on meaning,
which goes nowhere. So then I thought
that play was all there was to it —
not least because, out wandering,
I've seen the red-tailed hawks I love
scream in midair on windy days
until, God-like, the male bird tucks
his wings and plummets toward his mate.
A scant half-second before he hits,
he spreads wing and zooms off. Repeatedly
he feints, then veers, as I watch noon
sunlight glow red through his tail feathers.
And once, as he bore down, I saw
the female flip. The two locked talons
and tumbled almost to the pines before
they separated and the game
resumed. Courtship! I loved it once.
But who could bear it every spring?
Well, Mary could. "Don't be so serious,"
she says. But play is not enough.
I'm of at least two minds — like one
strange salamander that I found.
These salamanders breed too fast
to do it well — three tails, six legs.
With heads at either end, it crawled
one way until that end collapsed,
and then the other end would crawl
the other way — till it collapsed.

I tried to let it go. But how
could it escape? I tossed it back
into the mud and left it there, alive
when I walked off, but after that,
who knows? I'm stuck with stories now.
Perhaps this is a better one:
Along the Chattahoochee's bank,
I saw green cankerworms, in thousands,
moil — seethe — beneath the cottonwoods
like fat, green, severed fingers searching
for their lost hands. A scene of hell,
one Dante overlooked. But later,
at night, I went again and found
the cankerworms were gone. Instead
an equal number of dust-brown
moths fluttered over water. They
turned white, then silver, transformed
by moonlight. Exquisite. I left before
the magic turned them back to moths.

But here, lost, when I could get lost,
I loved the idea of mosquitoes,
lice, and ticks living off my blood,
as I lived off the meaning of the marsh.
Or off its lack of meaning — back
and forth. Mosquitoes, ticks: I loved
them as ideas. I never felt
so thoroughly that I was just
a soul and nothing else than when
my body fed their bodies. But,
dammit, the actual fact of them
was more than I could bear. *They hurt.*
But I've told Mary what to do

with facts: smack them around, and see
if they will tell you anything.
Some do. Some don't. Some waffle. Hell,
she's not convinced.
                        In winter light,
the marsh is stark, abstract. Just up
and down. The hard-edged light is clear,
incisive as a razor blade.
In summer, that same light smears everything.
Trees waver. Bushes merge into
a haze of gnats, shimmering in air,
which shimmers too — the whole world dizzy
and unsure. Meaning falls away.
The brilliant winter light, which then
made everything seem clear, now lies.
Or for the first time tells the truth.
Who cares? I do. But Mary loves me
whether I'm hawk, worm, salamander,
moth, tick, or just a confused man,
apprentice to himself, who fails
to grasp the meaning for the light,
although he loves them both: the winter light,
the summer light. And Mary too.

He Imagines His Wife Dead

I'd just leapt quickly to the curb
to keep from being run down by a horse,
when suddenly I understood my wife might die,
and since that time I've thought of little else,
as if the threatened mind is trying
to keep from being taken by surprise.
And worse, it tries to find the benefits:
the joys of flirting and games of courtship —
all things I loved but have no use for now.
How can I blame the mind? It wants to live
and will be ruthless to that end,
as a plant that's moved into a darkened room
will drop the lower, inessential leaves
to keep the growing tip alive. But the heart
depends on more than blood. It needs a cause.
I left my dull heart beating when I slept,
and found it beating when I woke
to Mary smiling oddly in her fever
as she lay tangled in the sweaty sheets.
Her eyes, unfocused and afraid,
were a blue I'd never seen in eyes before,
as if a jay were caught inside her head
and through her eyes I saw it leaping back and forth
and trying to extend its bright blue wings.
It scared me more than prison camp or war.
My Mary is my only love
that's not a subterfuge for death.

Dying

The pistol underneath my head
is cold. On August nights, it seems
the only cold thing in the world.
Life's dangerous out here, in woods,
and I don't even have the lungs
to play my flute. No tune I know
is simple, slow, and tremulous enough
to fit my breath. Which means, of course,
the pistol is a waste of time.
I'm not sure I could lift the stupid thing.
But I'm content to feel the iron
beneath my pillow: protector of the hearth,
defender of Confederate womanhood,
et cetera — a role I play
for Mary, who loves me, who'll grieve,
who loved me back before I knew
the heart — a hammer, anvil, forge —
could hold our flaws, and burn and beat them
into something useful: from sin
to virtue, battlefield to garden,
and suffering to grace, somehow.
Well, anyway, that's my best theory.

When we still lived, up to our necks
in debt, on Denmead Street, I'd loll
back in the tub and read the paper.
The water cooled. I'd holler, "Mary!"
She'd lug in boiling water, dump
it in the tub, go boil some more,

as if I could deserve such care.
What did I do for her? I made her laugh.

We had a fat tomcat who loved her
as if she were his god. He watched
her as she slept, left headless squirrels
and sparrows by the door; and when
she swept, he stalked the dust balls, pounced,
so Mary could admire his skills.
The afternoon that we conceived
our youngest — Rob — we rose from sex
and found the goddamned cat had sprayed my socks.
He cowered underneath the bed,
while I, down on my hands and knees,
swatted at him with my wet socks,
till Mary kicked my lifted rear.
My head smacked the bed frame. The cat
raced off and Mary laughed. Me too.
Two years. My lungs have been so weak
we last made love two years ago.

I think of this because this afternoon
she tilted my head back into her lap
and spread my hair across the blue
cloth of her dress. Slowly, with Job's
long patience, she combed through my head,
picking through each dark, separate strand,
finding the lice and crushing them,
one by one, beneath her fingernail.
Such life that clings to me! Such death
it takes to keep my body clean!
This is the greatest gift: to know
that someone sees you as you are

and loves you anyway. She must
have seen them when, last night, she slipped
into my dark tent and pulled off
her sweater. Sparks crackled, flew. In bed,
she pressed that fierce, electric body
— more full of light than it could hold —
against my flesh. And it responded.
My Lord, I didn't think it could.
She hiked her dress and mounted me.
I never saw her body, just felt
the moist engulfing of my flesh,
the holding deep inside, unmoving: me,
unable to move; her, still choosing not to,
a long time. Sobs broke from her mouth,
sweat soaked her dark blue dress, and she
rode me as I would ride a horse I loved,
knowing the orders that I carried
were more important than the horse,
and knowing, too, it didn't matter
whether the flailed horse lived. She fell
exhausted, on my face. Too weak
to push her off, I breathed her rich
sweat smell and tasted its faint salt.
She pressed her lips against my ear
and said, "I'm sorry." I said it back.
The words were not exactly right
but we both needed to forgive
our lives — and be forgiven. We'd touched
the big death with the little one,
the way, on entering a woman,
a sentimental man might pause
a long time, simply being there,
inside, knowing he'll soon begin

to move, withdraw, re-enter her
until he comes. But he might first
hold still as long as possible
before — at last, inevitably —
he starts to move, knowing that first
loves last, caresses it, and enters
and enters it again, till, awed,
they merge in elegiac shuddering.

But since I, breathless, couldn't move, she moved.

The Hereafter

Some people as they die grow fierce, afraid.
They see a bright light, offer frantic prayers,
and try to climb them, like Jacob's ladder, up
to heaven. Others, never wavering,
inhabit heaven years before they die,
so certain of their grace they can describe,
down to the gingerbread around the eaves,
the cottage God has saved for them. For hours
they'll talk of how the willow will not weep,
the flowering Judas not betray. They'll talk
of how they'll finally learn to play the flute
and speak good French.
              Still others know they'll rot
and their flesh turn to earth, which will become
live oaks, spreading their leaves in August light.
The green cathedral glow that shines through them
will light grandchildren playing hide-and-seek
inside the grove. My next-door neighbor says
he's glad the buzzards will at last give wings
to those of us who've envied swifts as they
swoop, twist, and race through tight mosquito runs.

And some — my brother's one — anticipate
the grave as if it were a chair pulled up
before a fire on winter nights. His ghost,
he thinks, will slouch into the velvet cushion,
a bourbon and branch water in its hand.
I've even met a man who says the soul
will come back in another skin — the way

a renter moves from house to house. Myself,
I'd like to come back as my father's hound.
Or something fast: a deer, a rust-red fox.

For so long I have thought of us as nails
God drives into the oak floor of this world,
it's hard to comprehend the hammer turned
to claw me out. I'm joking, mostly. I love
the possibilities — not one or two
but all of them. So if I had to choose,
pick only one and let the others go,
my death would be less strange, less rich, less like
a dizzying swig of fine rotgut. I roll
the busthead, slow, across my tongue and taste
the copper coils, the mockingbird that died
from fumes and plunged, wings spread, into the mash.
And underneath it all, just barely there,
I find the scorched-nut hint of corn that grew
in fields I walked, flourished beneath a sun
that warmed my skin, swaying in a changing wind
that tousled, stung, caressed, and toppled me.

From

THE NEVER-ENDING
(1991)

How Shall We Sing the Lord's Song
in a Strange Land?

We crept up, watched a black
man shovel dry bursts of dirt
into the air. Engrossed,
he didn't see me till
my friend hawked hard and then
stepped out of sight. The man
jerked back, convinced I meant
to spit on him. Held there
by guilt that wasn't fairly mine,
I braced for what he'd say.
Instead, he smiled, forgave
the sin I hadn't sinned,
and turned back to his work.
I stumbled off and yelled,
Goddamn you! at my friend,
who laughed. Behind us, sand
exploded from the hole, caught wind,
and drifted slowly down
past headstones. Within a month
two boys found the black man hanging
from a hickory, his face
vague in a mist of gnats.
And every time they told the story
the gnats grew thicker, fiercer.
But I believed. I ached
the guiltless ache of dreams
and shuddered. A family that
I never saw mourned him.

Their lives changed and that change
spread out past my small-boy
imagining — though I
tried hard to follow it,
at twelve already remembering
how, ten years old, I'd stand
before the mirror and aim
a flashlight in my mouth.
White cheeks glowed red. I knew
that when I flicked the switch
I would no longer shine
with bloodlight, like stained glass.
I would return to the flesh
I'd always been. Back then,
I thought that if I could
I'd forgive nothing — I'd
change everything. But that's
before I learned how we
get trapped inside the haunts
and habits of this world.
While we drink coffee, gossip,
my cousin's daughter pounds on
the piano. It drives me nuts.
But Ellen's used to it.
The child plays till she drops,
and then we lug her
— elongated and limp — to bed.
My cousin tucks her in,
chooses one music box
from dozens on a shelf, winds it,
and sets it by her child's
damp head. The girl hums, drifts
from one world she creates

into another. A dark
circle of drool surrounds her head.
My cousin loves her with
the tenderness we save
for something that will ruin
our lives, break us, nail
us irretrievably
into this world, which we,
like good philosophers,
had meant to hate. This world,
this world is home. But it
will never feel like home.

The Cestello Annunciation

The angel has already said, *Be not afraid.*
He's said, *The power of the Most High*
will darken you. Her eyes are downcast and half closed.
And there's a long pause — a pause here of forever —
as the angel crowds her. She backs away,
her left side pressed against the picture frame.

He kneels. He's come in all unearthly innocence
to tell her of glory — not knowing, not remembering
how terrible it is. And Botticelli
gives her eternity to turn, look out the doorway, where
on a far hill floats a castle, and halfway across
the river toward it juts a bridge, not completed —

and neither is the touch, angel to virgin,
both her hands held up, both elegant, one raised
as if to say *stop,* while the other hand, the right one,
reaches toward his; and, as it does, it parts her blue robe
and reveals the concealed red of her inner garment
to the red tiles of the floor and the red folds

of the angel's robe. But her whole body pulls away.
Only her head, already haloed, bows,
acquiescing. And though she will, she's not yet said,
Behold, I am the handmaid of the Lord,
as Botticelli, in his great pity,

lets her refuse, accept, refuse, and think again.

The Ugly Flowers

The brown fields freeze, unfreeze.
Because there's little else
to love in March, I love
the ugly flowers — coarse,
unlovely things that stink:
wild ginger, skunk cabbage,
and stinking benjamin.
Though rank as rotten meat
and though they mimic spring-
thawed carcasses, they bloom
first — even if they bloom
the purple-brown of carrion.
That's what it takes to blossom
when earth thaws soft one day
and freezes hard the next.
But they don't hold our love.
Next come — still earlier
even than the bees — coltsfoot
and dandelion before
narcissus, daffodil,
and jonquil rise and dazzle us
like perfect Christs at Easter —
each one returned from death,
untouched by it, in glory.
And who remembers then
wild ginger, skunk cabbage,
and stinking benjamin,
and how we loved them when

they bloomed amid brown grass,
churned mud — the unloved loved,
the death-plant beautiful.

Praying Drunk

Our Father who art in heaven, I am drunk.
Again. Red wine. For which I offer thanks.
I ought to start with praise, but praise
comes hard to me. I stutter. Did I tell you
about the woman whom I taught, in bed,
this prayer? It starts with praise; the simple form
keeps things in order. I hear from her sometimes.
Do you? And after love, when I was hungry,
I said, *Make me something to eat.* She yelled,
Poof! You're a casserole! — and laughed so hard
she fell out of the bed. Take care of her.

Next, confession — the dreary part. At night
deer drift from the dark woods and eat my garden.
They're like enormous rats on stilts except,
of course, they're beautiful. But why? What *makes*
them beautiful? I haven't shot one yet.
I might. When I was twelve, I'd ride my bike
out to the dump and shoot the rats. It's hard
to kill your rats, our Father. You have to use
a hollow point and hit them solidly.
A leg is not enough. The rat won't pause.
Yeep! Yeep! it screams, and scrabbles, three-legged, back
into the trash, and I would feel a little bad
to kill something that wants to live
more savagely than I do, even if
it's just a rat. My garden's vanishing.
Perhaps I'll merely plant more beans, though that
might mean more beautiful and hungry deer.

Who knows?

    I'm sorry for the times I've driven
home past a black, enormous, twilight ridge.
Crested with mist, it looked like a giant wave
about to break and sweep across the valley,
and in my loneliness and fear I've thought,
O let it come and wash the whole world clean.
Forgive me. This is my favorite sin: despair —
whose love I celebrate with wine and prayer.

Our Father, thank you for all the birds and trees,
that nature stuff. I'm grateful for good health,
food, air, some laughs, and all the other things
I'm grateful that I've never had to do
without. I have confused myself. I'm glad
there's not a rattrap large enough for deer.
While at the zoo last week, I sat and wept
when I saw one elephant insert his trunk
into another's ass, pull out a lump,
and whip it back and forth impatiently
to free the goodies hidden in the filth.
I could have let it mean most anything,
but I was stunned again at just how little
we ask for in our lives. *Don't look! Don't look!*
Two young nuns tried to herd their giggling
schoolkids away. *Line up,* they called. *Let's go
and watch the monkeys in the monkey house.*
I laughed, and got a dirty look. Dear Lord,
we lurch from metaphor to metaphor,
which is — let it be so — a form of praying.

I'm usually asleep by now — the time
for supplication. Requests. As if I'd stayed

up late and called the radio and asked
they play a sentimental song. Embarrassed.
I want a lot of money and a woman.
And, also, I want vanishing cream. You know —
a character like Popeye rubs it on
and disappears. Although you see right through him,
he's there. He chuckles, stumbles into things,
and smoke that's clearly visible escapes
from his invisible pipe. It makes me think,
sometimes, of you. What makes me think of me
is the poor jerk who wanders out on air
and then looks down. Below his feet, he sees
eternity, and suddenly his shoes
no longer work on nothingness, and down
he goes. As I fall past, remember me.

Bewilderments of the Eye

My neighbor's bug light sizzles beyond the hedge
until I want to scream. A loud, wild shriek
would serve the bastard right for all the death
he's meting out. Oh, sure, it's only bugs,
but when you're down you pity even them.
My self-indulgent soul leads me to pray,
God bless the moth, whose nervous system just
says *light, light, light, light, light* — the thing it loves.
I've learned to gauge the noise and estimate
what bug is zapped. Large ones fight back. Mosquitoes
disintegrate in one electric snap.

The thin, sweet smell of Malathion drifts
over the hedge. Some folks can't take the world,
its flaws. My neighbor's one and so am I,
although I lack his energy. Young swifts,
attracted by the bugs, have fallen in
the blue current. Sometimes they make it out.
It's fifty-fifty live or die, I'd guess.

Idly, I slap mosquitoes as they land,
and if they leave a spot of blood, it's shared:
once mine, then theirs, now mine again. The moths,
when I go in and douse the light, possess

no purpose in their lives, not even death,
beating into the darkness and the trees,
where they don't want to fly — as once, sleepless,
I stood right here and watched the opposite:
two barn owls flying hard across the dawn,
no longer hunting, hurrying toward darkness,
paler, paler, till they disappeared
in the failure of my eyes in too much light.

Two Ember Days in Alabama

1.

Out with my dog at dawn — we couldn't sleep —
I met a woman hanging laundry, mist
rising from warm, wet clothes. The empty forms
flapped on the line like pieces of three ghosts
filling with wind before they froze. And further on,
in woods, I saw the vaguely hourglass shape
my boot had stamped in mud the day before,
and, frozen in it, the hoofprint of a deer.
Dan sniffed it, whined, jerked at the leash, his nose
aimed low into the brambled underbrush.
We circled home past bright clothes frozen stiff.
Like pendulums, they ticktocked in the wind.

I shivered underneath cold, rumpled sheets
and so did Dan, who warmed my feet. At noon
we didn't budge. Rain, like a gray hammer, fell.
By now my footprints and the deer's have merged
in mud, the wild spring loosening of earth.

2.

My tomcats saunter from near woods, and when
I hold them, resisting, up against my cheek
I smell — what is it? Smoke, confused with fur.
And now, in deepest Lent, an Ember Day,
I marvel at the inconclusive whiff of fire
that lingers there. This Lent, too, lingers on
like twilight or the study of last things.
The blackbirds peck through dried-up winter weeds.

There's nothing much to eat that I can see,
but they are fat and glossy as eight balls.
As I walk out the door, they rise and join
the northward stream of blackbirds, grackles, crows
that have for days been building energy
for exodus. They've swelled the barren woods,
loading the unleaved trees like the black fruit
of nothingness. And now they simply leave.
First fall, then winter. Then this long pause. And then
the starting over. And then the never-ending.

Heat Lightning in a Time of Drought

My neighbor, drunk, stood on his lawn and yelled,
Want some! Want some! He bellowed it as cops
cuffed him, shoved him in their back seat — *Want some!* —
and drove away. Now I lie here awake,
not by choice, listening to the crickets' high
electric trill, urgent with lust. Heat lightning flashes.
The crickets will not, will not stop. I wish
that I could shut the window, pull the curtain, sleep.
But it's too hot. *Want some!* He screamed it till
I was afraid I'd made him up to scream
what I knew better than to say out loud
although it's August-hot and every move
bathes me in sweat and we are careless,
careless, careless, every one of us,
and when my neighbor screams out in his yard
like one dog howling for another dog,
I call the cops, then lie in my own sweat,
remembering the woman
who, at a party on a night this hot,
walked up to me, propped her chin on my chest,
and sighed. She was a little drunk, the love-light
unshielded in her eyes. We fell in love.
One day at supper the light fixture dropped,
exploded on the table. Glass flew around us,
a low, slow-motion blossoming of razors.
She was unhurt till I reached out my hand
— left hand — to brush glass from her face.
Two drops of blood ran down her cheek.
On TV, I'd seen a teacher dip a rose

in liquid nitrogen. When he withdrew it,
it smoked, frozen solid. He snapped one petal, frail
as isinglass, and then, against the table,
he shattered it. The whole rose blew apart.
Like us. And then one day the doorbell rang.
A salesman said, *Watch this!* He stripped my bed
and vacuumed it. The nozzle sucked up two
full, measured cups of light gray flakes. He said,
That's human skin. I stood, refusing the purchase,
stood staring at her flesh and mine commingled
inside the measuring cup, stood there and thought,
She's been gone two years, she's married, and all this time
her flesh has been in bed with me. Don't laugh.
Don't laugh. That's what the Little Moron says
when he arrives home early from a trip
and finds his wife in bed with someone else.
The man runs off. The Little Moron puts
a pistol to his own head, cocks the hammer.
His wife, in bed, sheets pulled up to her chin,
starts laughing. *Don't you laugh!* he screams. *Don't laugh —*
you're next. It is the wisest joke I know because
the heart's a violent muscle, opening
and closing. Who knows what we might do:
by night, the craziness of dreams; by day,
the craziness of logic. Listen!
My brother told me of a man wheeled, screaming,
into the ward, a Pepsi bottle rammed
up his ass. I was awed: there is no telling
what we'll do in our fierce drive to come together.
The heart keeps opening and closing like a mine
where fire still burns, a century underground,
following the veins of black coal, rearing up
to take a barn, a house, a pasture. Although

I wish that it would rain tonight, I fret
about the heat lightning that flicks and glitters
on the horizon as if it promised rain.
It can't. But I walk outside, stand on parched grass,
and watch it hungrily — all light, all dazzle —
remembering how we'd drive out past the town's light,
sit on the hood, and watch great thunderheads
huge as a state — say, Delaware — sail past. Branched
lightning jagged, burst the dark from zenith to horizon.
We stared at almost nothing: some live oaks,
the waist-high corn. Slow raindrops smacked the corn,
plopped in the dirt around us, drummed the roof,
and finally reached out, tapped us on the shoulders.
We drove home in the downpour, laughed, made love
— still wet with rain — and slept. But why stop there?
Each happy memory leads me to a sad one:
the friend who helped me through my grief by drinking
all of my liquor. And when, at last, we reached
the wretched mescal, he carefully sliced off
the worm's black face, ate its white body, staggered
onto this very lawn, and racked and heaved
until I helped him up. *You're okay, John.*
You've puked it out. "No, man — you're wrong. That worm
ain't ever coming out." Heat lightning flashes.
No rain falls and no thunder cracks the heat.
No first concussion dwindles to a long
low rolling growl. I go in the house, lie down,
pray, masturbate, drift to the edge of sleep.
I wish my soul were larger than it is.

The Yellow Harvest

After last harvest, as the trees blaze orange,
three peasant women trudge
through stubble fields and kneel, heads bowed,
before the yellow Christ. On their stripped field,

Gauguin has painted his last cross
and nailed himself to it. Gauguin:
there's no mistaking that thin beard, that face,
that tilt of head. But he's no longer Paul Gauguin.

Bright yellow tinged with green — the color
of the autumn fields stretched out behind him —
he's Christ. He's harvested: cut, bundled,
and, like a last shock of late wheat,

left in the field past gathering.
And this Christ knows he's dying. He yearns
to return — to bloom, seed, wither, die,
and come again. The women gathered at his feet

pray to endure the winter, pray
to eat, keep warm, and prosper. But Christ,
who was once Paul Gauguin,
sags on his cross. The yellow hills,

the yellow valley, and the gleaned
dry yellow hills — all dying — call,
O Son of Man, we're coming back.
Put down your soul and follow us.

In the Game

From deep left field, I watch the hitter.
Then, bored, I watch a hawk, tip feathers
adjusting as he hunts. Air jolts.
Flatcars jerk past. From underneath thick netting,
artillery splotched with camouflage
aims past our playing field. I turn
and gawk, awed by the huge green weapons,
as if I had forgotten somehow
the necessary violences
that let us play our game. Behind me
my brother yells, *Get in the game!*
It's late. I think we're two runs down.
Mike charges a weak grounder, whips
the ball to first. Out three, thank God.
As I jog across the parched infield,
the slow train churns the air
explosively and I remember when
Mike ran home from a ball game, fell
on the front lawn, heat-struck, and thrashed
until I leapt across his chest. He yelled,
Don't let me hurt anybody! but a wild
blow clipped my cheek and, shit, I slammed
my fist, twice, hard — into his ribs.
We fought till Momma turned the hose on us.
Mike pushed himself free, walked, embarrassed,
into the house. He has, of course,
hurt others — as I, by telling this,
hurt him again to help myself
toward understanding, a vicious truth

and one I cannot do without
though I don't care to think about it,
like this slow military train
that jolts into the distance. Green, tan,
and olive splotches blend with pines,
invisible. I cannot tell
exactly where they merge, become
the same thing. Natural and unnatural —
I used to be so sure which one
was which. The umpire calls strike one
while I stand stupid, thinking. But then
I bear down, double to right. Mike tears
past third, slides hard, and sends the catcher sprawling.
He yells. Mike yells back, shoves. I edge off second,
judging the steal. We're one behind,
with one man, me, on base.

Elegy for My Father, Who Is Not Dead

One day I'll lift the telephone
and be told my father's dead. He's ready.
In the sureness of his faith, he talks
about the world beyond this world
as though his reservations have
been made. I think he wants to go,
a little bit — a new desire
to travel building up, an itch
to see fresh worlds. Or older ones.
He thinks that when I follow him
he'll wrap me in his arms and laugh,
the way he did when I arrived
on earth. I do not think he's right.
He's ready. I am not. I can't
just say goodbye as cheerfully
as if he were embarking on a trip
to make my later trip go well.
I see myself on deck, convinced
his ship's gone down, while he's convinced
I'll see him standing on the dock
and waving, shouting, *Welcome back.*

Compost: An Ode

Who can bring a clean thing out of an unclean?
—JOB 14:4

The beauty of the compost heap is not
the eye's delight.
                Eyes see too much.
                        They see
blood-colored worms
            and bugs so white they seem
to feed off ghosts. Eyes
             do not see the heat
that simmers in
          the moist heart of decay —
in its unmaking,
         making fire,
             just hot
enough to burn
         itself. In summer, the heap
burns like a stove. It can — almost — hurt you.
I've held my hand inside the fire and counted
one, two, three,
        four.
           I cannot hold it there.
Give it to me, the heat insists. *It's mine.*
I yank it back and wipe it on my jeans
as if
    I'd really heard the words.
              And eyes
cannot appreciate
         sweet vegetable rot,

how good it smells
                        as everything dissolves,
dispersing
                back from thing
                            into idea.

From our own table we are feeding it
what we don't eat. Orange rind and apple core,
corn husks,
                  and odds and ends the children smear
across their plates — we feed them all into the slow,
damp furnace of decay. Leaves curl at edges,
buckle,
             collapsing down into their centers,
as everything turns loose its living shape
and blackens, gives up
                      what it once was
to become dirt. The table scraps
and leafage join,
                 indistinguishable,
the way that death insists it's all the same,
while life
             must do a million things at once.
The compost heap is both — life, death — a slow
simmer,
            a leisurely collapsing of
the thing
             into its possibilities —
both bean and hollyhock, potato, zinnia, squash:
the opulence
               of everything that rots.

The Unpromised Land

Montgomery, Alabama

Despite the noon sun shimmering on Court Street,
each day I leave my desk, and window-shop,
waste time, and use my whole lunch hour to stroll
the route the marchers took. The walk is blistering —
the kind of heat that might make you recall
Nat Turner skinned and rendered into grease
if you share my cheap liberal guilt for sins
before your time. I hold it dear. I know
if I had lived in 1861
I would have fought in butternut, not blue,
and never known I'd sinned. Nat Turner skinned
for doing what I like to think I'd do
if I were him.

                        Before the war
half-naked coffles were paraded to Court Square,
where Mary Chesnut gasped — "seasick" — to see
a bright mulatto on the auction block,
who bantered with the buyers, sang bawdy songs,
and flaunted her green satin dress, smart shoes.
I'm sure the poor thing knew who'd purchase her,
wrote Mrs. Chesnut, who plopped on a stool
to discipline her thoughts. Today I saw,
in that same square, three black girls pick loose tar,
flick it at one another's new white dresses,
then squeal with laughter. Three girls about the age
of those blown up in church in Birmingham.

The legendary buses rumble past the church
where Reverend King preached when he lived in town,
a town somehow more his than mine, despite
my memory of standing on Dexter Avenue
and watching, fascinated, a black man fry
six eggs on his Dodge Dart. Because I watched
he gave me one with flecks of dark blue paint
stuck on the yolk. My mother slapped my hand.
I dropped the egg. And when I tried to say
I'm sorry, Mother grabbed my wrist and marched me
back to our car.

        I can't hold to the present.
I've known these streets, their history, too long.
Two months before she died, my grandmother
remembered when I'd sassed her as a child,
and at the dinner table, in midbite,
leaned over, struck the grown man on the mouth.
And if I hadn't said *I'm sorry*, fast,
she would have gone for me again. My aunt,
from laughing, choked on a piece of lemon pie.
But I'm not sure. I'm just Christian enough
to think each sin taints every one of us,
a harsh philosophy that doesn't seem
to get me very far — just to the Capitol
each day at noon, my wet shirt clinging to my back.
Atop its pole, the Stars and Bars,
too heavy for the breeze, hangs listlessly.

Once, standing where Jeff Davis took his oath,
I saw the crippled governor wheeled into
the Capitol. He shrank into his chair,
so flaccid with paralysis he looked

like melting flesh, white as a maggot. He's fatter now.
He courts black votes, and life is calmer than
when Muslims shot whites on this street, and calmer
than when the Klan blew up Judge Johnson's house
or Martin Luther King's. My history could be worse.
I could be Birmingham. I could be Selma.
I could be Philadelphia, Mississippi.

Instead, I'm this small river town. Today,
as I worked at my desk, the boss
called to the janitor, *Jerome, I hear
you get some lunchtime pussy every day.*
Jerome, toothless and over seventy,
stuck the broom handle out between his legs:
Yessir! When the Big Hog talks
— he waggled the broomstick — *I gots to listen.*
He laughed. And from the corner of his eye,
he looked to see if we were laughing too.

New Headstones at the Shelby Springs
Confederate Cemetery

Though wild, each flower has its name:
sweet william, dogtooth violet,
wild iris, wild geranium.
Some of the headstones, too, bear names:
Rucks, Murphry, Bookout. Mostly, though,
it's *Unknown Soldier CSA*.

It's late. At dusk, cool slanted light
glows opalescent on white stones,
and at the end of a long row
we stand and talk about — what else? —
mortality: unknown, a name,
unknown, me, you, and you.

                         I snap
a green weed from a grave and chew it
for its sharp, sour burst of juice.
One of you — which? — breaks off a stalk
and says, "Sheep sorrel."

                    It's *sorrel?* Sorrel!
She's dead and buried — and all my life
I'd heard my mother say *sheep sorrow*.
Now her teaching voice comes back
and says it slowly, properly
— *sheep sorrel* — so I will get it right.

But even she can't name these men
whose namelessness is now engraved
in marble. Adam had it easy.
He merely had to name the world's
ephemera, while we have to
remember it. Sheep sorrel, yes!
Wild iris, wood sage, chicory,
sweet william, Sarah, Norman, me,
and some red spiky thing, which blooms
at our feet as we walk back home.

Roberta was my mother's name.

Christ as a Gardener

The boxwoods planted in the park spell LIVE.
I never noticed it until they died.
Before, the entwined green had smudged the word
unreadable. And when they take their own advice
again — come spring, come Easter — no one will know
a word is buried in the leaves. I love
that Mary thought her resurrected Lord
a gardener. It wasn't just the broad-brimmed hat
and muddy robe that fooled her: he was *that* changed.
He looks across the unturned field, the riot
of unscythed grass, the smattering of wildflowers.
Before he can stop himself, he's on his knees.
He roots up stubborn weeds, pinches the suckers,
deciding order here — what lives, what dies,
and how. But it goes deeper even than that.
His hands burn and his bare feet smolder. He longs
to lie down inside the long, dew-moist furrows
and press his pierced side and his broken forehead
into the dirt. But he's already done it —
passed through one death and out the other side.
He laughs. He kicks his bright spade in the earth
and turns it over. Spring flashes by, then harvest.
Beneath his feet, seeds dance into the air.
They rise, and he, not noticing, ascends
on midair steppingstones of dandelion,
of milkweed, thistle, cattail, and goldenrod.

Communion in the Asylum

We kneel. Some of us kneel better than others
and do not have to clutch the rail or sway
against those next to us. We hold up hands
to take the body in, and some of our hands
— a few — are firmer than the others. They
don't tremble, don't have to be held in the priest's
encircling hands and guided to our lips.
And some of us can hold the wafer, all of it,
inside our mouths. And when the careful priest
tips wine across our lips, many of us, for reverence,
don't moan or lurch or sing songs to ourselves.
But we all await the grace that's promised us.

Psalm Against Psalms

Unto the pure all things are pure.

God had Isaiah eat hot coals,
Ezekiel eat shit, and they sang
his praises. I've eaten neither, despite
my childhood need to test most things
inside my mouth. My brothers and I
popped small frogs over our lips.
They'd crouch in the close dark, then bump,
tickling, against the roofs of our mouths.
We'd brace, try not to laugh, because
the winner was the one who last
spit out his frog. Actually,
it's not my story. It happened
to a woman who told it to me
right after I leaned over, kissed her.
But I think it is my memory
because I wish it were — as I
have thought of shit and fire and what
they'd taste like in my mouth. Kids jam the world,
hand over fist, into their mouths,
but fire only once, shit only once.
And even pregnant women, who,
where I come from, will eat red clay,
not knowing they eat it for the iron,
just knowing something drives them out
into the fields to eat earth — secret,
furtive, ashamed — do not eat fire.
Smokers smoke, pulling the fire closer

and closer to their lips, but no one,
except by accident, pulls it
into his mouth. A few professionals
pretend to eat the blossom off a torch,
and then exhale a violent billowing,
like a soul blasting from the flesh
that cannot hold it. And I have even heard
of a man, who, in a darkened kitchen,
turned all the burners on and watched
orange spirals floating in the dark,
shimmering like elaborate UFOs. He watched
until he couldn't hold back any longer;
and he climbed on the counter, pressed
his naked chest against the spirals
as if he could embrace the fire, love it,
consume the burning, and not be burnt.

Isaiah ate the blood-red ember.
Ezekiel ate the dung. It went in fire
and came out praise. It went in shit
and came praise from his mouth. And this
is where I stick. I pray: thank, ask,
confess. But praise — dear God! — it clings
like something dirty on my tongue,
like shit. Or burns because it is a lie.
And yet I try: I pray and ask
for praise, then force the balking words
out of my mouth as if the saying them
could form the glowing coal — cool,
smooth as a ruby — on my tongue.
Or mold inside my mouth the shit
that melts like caramel — and thereby,
by magic, change my heart. Instead

I croak the harsh begrudging praise
of those who conjure grace, afraid
that it might come, afraid it won't.
But if grace tore through me and spoke,
as God in his strange redundant way
put on my tongue to praise himself,
I'd hear the words I said and learn
why I invented all the horrors of the world,
learn why I made us humans love
our hard sweet lives, then added death
to give it all intensity.

When she dropped food, my mother scooped
it from the floor, flicked off the grit,
blew on it, and pronounced it clean
before she put it on my plate.
I do the same. And when I cut my hand,
I jam the finger in my mouth
and suck my own blood, hot and salty
as melted butter. I'm not fastidious
between extremes of fire and shit — the one
so pure it smolders on our flesh,
the other one so pure our flesh
refuses it, expels it, walks away.
That's why so few of us are prophets.
God-like, they feast on purities,
pure spirit or pure excrement.
I'm smaller, human, in between,
a leavening of dirt with fire.
And I must be, with every passing day,
more careful of what goes into my mouth,
more reckless of what issues forth.

From

THE GLASS HAMMER
(1994)

The Glass Hammer

My mother's knickknack crystal hammer
shone on the shelf. "Put that thing down.
It's not a play-pretty." *Tap, tap*
against my wooden blocks. "I said,
PUT   THAT   THING   DOWN!"

But when she wasn't looking — ha! —
I'd sneak back to the hammer, and heft it.
Enchanted, I held it to my eyes
and watched, through it, the living room
shift, waver, and go shimmery — haloed

with hidden fire. Our worn green sofa glowed
and lost its shape, as if some deeper shape
were trying to break loose. The chairs,
the walls, the cross-stitched pictures all
let go, smeared into one another.

I scrounged a rust-flecked nail, and hit it.
The hammer shattered in my hand.
Blood spattered on my shorts. I screamed,
was snatched off my fat bloody feet,
rushed to the doctor, stitched, cooed at, spanked,

embraced, told *never, never, never
do that again,* and pondered how
I could, the hammer having burst,
and not, therefore, a proper hammer
despite the gorgeous world it held.

My Father's Corpse

He lay stone still, pretended to be dead.
My brothers and I, tiny, swarmed over him
like puppies. He wouldn't move. We tickled him,
tracing our fingers up and down his huge
misshapen feet — then armpits, belly, face.
He wouldn't move. We pushed small fingers up
inside his nostrils, wiggled them, and giggled.
He wouldn't move. We peeled his eyelids back,
stared into those motionless, blurred circles. Still,
he wouldn't, didn't move. Then we, alarmed,
poked, prodded his great body urgently.
Diddy, are you okay? Are you okay?
He didn't move. I reared back, gathered speed,
and slammed my forehead on his face. He rose,
he rose up roaring, scattered us from his body
and, as he raged, we sprawled at his feet — thrilled
to have the resurrected bastard back.

Grandmother's Spit

To wipe the sleep grains from my eyes or rub
a food smudge from my cheek, Grandmother'd lick
her rough right thumb and order me, *Come here.*
She'd clutch my arm and hold me near her face
while, with that spit-damp thumb, she scrubbed the spot.
I struggled like a kitten being licked,
then leaned into the touch, again catlike,
helping that fierce thumb scour loose the dirt.
It smelled, her spit, of lipstick and tobacco —
breath-warm, enveloping. She'd hold me at arm's length,
peer hard into my face, and state, *You're clean.*
When she let go, I'd crouch behind the door
and, with my own spit, rub the clean spot raw.

Dog Pile

Somebody'd yell, "Dog pile on Andrew!" I'd drop
my homework and tear across the asphalt,
trying to make it to the grass. Somebody
tackled me and slammed me to the hardtop.
I gasped as each late boy flopped on the pile
and jarred my breath loose. Under the pile,
I was a little bruised, a little angry,
a little pleased they knew my name, which is only
one of the dangers of a name. "Get off me!"
I bellowed, and flailed at the slow ones. My friends
peeled off the pile and waited for me to choose.
I paused dramatically, looked around, and yelled,
"Dog pile on Hudgins!" First everybody froze,
and then my brother started running.

Haircut

"Quit sniveling! Sit still!" And in disgust
he palmed my head like a basketball
and forced it down and buzzed the clippers up
my neck again. Hair sifted down my collar.
I squirmed. He jerked the pink bath towel
tighter against my throat, and hair
flew up and landed in the sugar bowl.
Then gradually, to even out mistakes,
my hair grew shorter, more like stubble,
more like West Point or hot Fort Hood,
where I was born. We saved some money.
But now it's his turn and he sits,
hands folded on his lap, unsteady,
while I, with tiny scissors, snip
the gray hair curling from his nostrils
and from both ears; and, Jesus, at sixty
the death hairs really get their growth,
don't they? The scissors pinch his skin
and he tries not to flinch. "Sit still!"
I snarl, and I'm so horrified
I say it one more time. "Sit still."

Transistor Radio

Summer nights I huddled under
bed sheets in the hot dark
of my own breathing, ear pressed
against my father's radio.
This was forbidden: listening
to songs of cheating lovers,
lost unrecovered loves,
drink, song itself, and making
believe. I yearned and feared
to suffer that suffering
so the hurt would justify
my pure unhappiness,
at last. And now we march,
conscripts of sorrow who first
were volunteers. I hummed,
ignorant of what it meant:
walking the floor, you've got
that faraway look
in your eyes. But knowing that
I would find out, I sang
the forbidden words, ears pressed
to older worlds, in the hot
dark of my own slow breathing.

Fireflies After Twilight

The intermittent flick of light so quick
I wasn't sure it was light
but something my drowsy eye had tricked
out of its fear of darkness, which
pressed into the screened-in porch
where I lay watching, afraid, but not enough
to move back in the house, which sweltered:
the fireflies rose. Rarely more
than one light quavered at a time,
flicking its diminishing sexual light
against the crowded pines. Eros
and Thanatos I'll call it now,
but then I simply called it fear.
If I'm still frightened — and I am —
it's complicated with yearnings
toward doubleness and indecision:
how during sunlight I block light,
which warms my back and loosens me,
while after dark I stand out, white
against the black pines — usually
but not always at odds with nature,
God and the gods, whom I resisted
when I crushed fireflies on my cheeks.
a war paint of false light, then dashed
from moonbeam to tree shadow, stalking . . .
Not stalking anything, just stalking
till I was sleepy. The fireflies rise until
it's been a long time with no light
against the darkness. I'm gone, I'm nothing,
and then it's sunrise, morning, day.

Begotten

I've never, as some children do,
looked at my folks and thought, I *must*
have come from someone else —
rich parents who'd misplaced me, but
who would, as in a myth or novel,
return and claim me. Hell, no. I saw
my face in cousins' faces, heard
my voice in their high drawls. And Sundays,
after the dinner plates were cleared,
I lingered, elbow propped on red
oilcloth, and studied great-uncles, aunts,
and cousins new to me. They squirmed.
I stared till I discerned the features
they'd gotten from the family larder:
eyes, nose, lips, hair? I stared until,
uncomfortable, they'd snap, "Hey, boy —
what are you looking at? At me?"
"No, sir," I'd lie. "No, ma'am." I'd count ten
and then continue staring at them.
I never had to ask, What am I?
I stared at my blood-kin, and thought,
So *this*, dear God, is what I am.

Blue Danube

As we clung to the corner and catcalled,
Miz Caldwell waltzed her tall befuddled friend
across the room. When the record circled past
the last note, she twirled her partner to a halt.
The needle scraped. Miz Caldwell turned to us
and said, "A waltz — that's how it's done. You try!
One-two-three, one-two-three." And by her side
the taller woman blinked, swayed sleepily,
as if she'd just awakened. "Don't count steps. Glide!"
We tangled in our box steps, frustrated, and she,
frustrated too, shrieked, "No, no, no! This way!"
She locked her palm against her partner's back
and drove her hard across the floor, bent backward
in cha-cha-chas or held elegantly
erect in waltzes, so dedicated to the dance
she wouldn't stop and break it into steps
for us to follow. She didn't care. They danced,
and went somewhere we couldn't go, and left us
shuffling in the rec room of First Methodist,
flat-footed, untransported. Across their feet
we slithered pennies, nickels, and even dimes.
They didn't miss a step. The needle rose.
She pushed it down again — "Blue Danube" — and smiled,
smiled tightly. "You boys! Let's see what you have learned."

Magic Button

My uncle gouged a circle in the dirt,
then closed the knife against his thigh. "See that?
Let's say that circle there's a magic button.
Let's say nobody'd see you if you pressed it,
nobody'd ever know. But if you did,
the niggers all would disappear, like *that*."
He snapped his fingers.
                              "But that's murder!" I said.
"Nope. They wouldn't die. They'd disappear.
And all their nigger shit would go with them —
loud music, dope, and welfare." I tried again:
"Come on! It isn't like they stood in line
to ride those wonderful slave ships."
                                        "I know
how they got here. That's not what I'm discussing.
I'm only asking whether you'd press the button
if nobody'd know, nobody'd see. I would,"
he said, and ground his boot heel on the circle.
We stood there a long time, not talking, staring
at the deep circle cut into the dirt.

In Thomas Jefferson's first memory
a slave transports him on a silken pillow.

Thus

Before I went to bed, I'd show
my father what I'd done that night.
The work was always smudged. I'd strain
to set the problem up, then beat
the numbers into it. Hunched
over the kitchen table, I'd copy
each page until he said it looked
acceptable. *Quit sniffling,* he'd say.
I'll give you something real
to cry about. And he was right.
I knew, even then, I wasn't entitled
to misery. My father'd put his head
down close to mine and say,
softly, *You've never had to worry*
where your next meal is coming from.
What could I say? From algebra
I was learning Plato — nothing fancy —
learning that numbers were more cruel
than I could ever hope to be,
and I had hoped to be ruthless.

Jack

"I've got to pee." "I'm hungry." "I want to stop."
And Daddy jerked the car onto the shoulder.
"You want to get out? Okay, then — get out!"
We did, and he drove slowly out of sight,
watching the mirror. I started blubbering

but Jack just said, "Let's go." We marched,
and gravel crunched beneath our feet
till Daddy, laughing, roared back up. He laughed
at me for being so relieved, at Jack's
pretending not to care. But that was Jack.

When Daddy snapped his belt off, I started screaming.
Not Jack. We'd kneel across the sofa, butts
raised in the air, our pants around our ankles,
and while I bellowed, Jack gritted his teeth
and made no sound except the grunt or two

knocked out of him so Daddy couldn't say
"You're not hurt, you just think you are."
When we were small, I'd knock Jack to the ground
and kick him in the belly. He'd curl
around my foot and moan and, Jesus, I thought

I'd ruptured him. I'd crouch beside his head
and beg him not to tell. But he kept growing.
When Daddy laced us into boxing gloves
and shoved us at each other, I couldn't block
his hard, quick hands. I tried to cover up,

and Daddy, disgusted, smacked me to the ground.
This fighting business wasn't working out.
Last fight: Mom stepped between us as we yelled.
I reached around her head and popped him in the mouth.
"Please let me at him! Please!" he sobbed, and tried

to slide past Mom without touching her,
and I, sidestepping to keep her body between us,
yelled, "Come on. Yeah, come on, Mister Big Mouth!"
"You're brothers. You're supposed to love each other,"
Mom wailed. "Yeah, sure. On the Pollyanna planet."

I hoped I looked as crazy as he did,
hands snatching past her shoulders, grabbing for me,
till I pushed Mom aside, kicked at his balls,
missed, fought as best I could, and took my beating.

Colonel

My father lifts the crippled airman's body
and jokes about how light he is and how
we need some rain. He holds him while the man's
young wife strips off the yellowed linen, cracks
white sheets above the bed, and lets them drift
across the mattress. She smooths them, tucks the corner.
My father lays the shriveled Christian down.
Three times one week, four times the next. A job
he shares with someone from another church.
He comes home ashen. And every single time,
before he leaves the house he turns to me,
false casually, "You want to come along?"
"Do you need help?" I ask, and he says no.
He leaves. I watch TV. I'm sixteen, shit!
And I don't want to be a soldier yet.

At Work

The white woman steered her loaded cart aside,
out of the checkout lane: "You go ahead."
The drunk black woman snarled, "It's goddamn time
you white folks let us go ahead of you."
She threw her hips into the lane and slammed
a six-pack on the moving belt. Then: *thud!*

The colored woman, like a folding chair,
collapsed. And as she fell, I saw behind her
the stunned white woman holding half
a catsup bottle by the neck. She shrugged.
She looked past me, said "Niggers!," and began
unloading groceries by the register.

When I got home I told my mom. She said,
"I can't keep straight what they want to be called.
I wish they'd make their minds up." Grandmomma knew:
"Oh, negroes, nigras, colored, black — my God!
They're niggers and they know they're niggers too."

When the cops left I'd had to mop it up:
blood, catsup, glass. And since the mop was out,
the boss said hit the produce section too.
So by the time I dumped it down the drain,
the water, without a trace of red, frothed black,
just like it always did. But I enjoyed
slopping the dirty mop across the shoes
of customers who wouldn't move their feet.

Hunting with My Brother

My brother blasts pigeons beneath the bridge
and lets them lie. *They're only flying rats,*
he says, and just like Daddy I snap, "Two wrongs
don't make a right." *But two rights make a left,*
he says. We laugh, and talk of how his wife
cooks squirrels with dumplings and black pepper
and how my garden's gone to seed.

He swings the shotgun to his shoulder. Two quick
squirrels scrabble, spiraling up a water oak.
Frustrated, Jack fires into the ragged nests.
"Hey, knock it off," I yell. He shrugs,
twists up the choke, and fires again.
I grab the barrel and wrench it. His fist
clips my left ear. I cock my fist,
but we're already backing off,
apologizing.
        We hike two miles in silence.
Jack's wife looks from the kitchen window.
We hold up empty hands and shrug. She laughs.
We glare at her and, goddamn, she laughs louder.
Then slowly we laugh too. Who wouldn't laugh
at Cain and Abel coming home —
no meat, no beans, and both alive.

From

BABYLON IN A JAR
(1998)

The Chinaberry

I couldn't stand still watching them forever,
but when I moved
                        the grackles covering
each branch and twig
                        sprang
                                    together into flight
and for a moment in midair they held
the tree's shape,
                        the black tree
                                    peeling from the green,
as if
        they were its shadow or its soul, before
they scattered,
                        circled and
                                    re-formed
as grackles heading south for winter grain fields.
Oh, it
        was just a chinaberry tree,
the birds were simply grackles.
                                    A miracle
made from this world and where I stood in it.
But you can't know how long
                                    I stood there watching.
And you can't know how desperate I'd become
advancing
                        each step on the feet of my
advancing shadow,
                                    how bitter and afraid I was
matching step after step with the underworld,

my ominous, indistinct, and mirror image
darkening with
                    extreme and antic nothings
the ground I walked on,
                         inexact reversals,
elongated and foreshortened parodies
of each
         foot lowering itself
                         onto its shadow.
And you can't know how I had tried to force
the moment, make it happen
                         before it happened —
not necessarily this
                    though this is what I saw:
black birds deserting the tree they had become,
becoming,
         for a moment in midair,
the chinaberry's shadow for a moment
after they had ceased to be
                         the chinaberry,
then scattering:
                    meaning after meaning —
birds strewn across the morning like flung gravel
until
      they found themselves again as grackles,
found each other,
               found South
                         and headed there,
while I stood before
                    the green, abandoned tree.

Ashes

My left hand joggled Johnny's arm, and Johnny
— Jesus! —
             Johnny dropped the coffee can
holding his sister. The can
                   rolled jerkily,
the lid
      spun off, and Sister Rachel spilled
across the black linoleum.
Did I mention we'd been drinking? Everyone
stepped back,
          then back again.
                    Who wants
to track a woman's ashes on the floor
of a rented hall, then get home
                 slightly drunk,
pull off his dress shoes and find a residue
of fine dust
        trapped in the polished leather creases,
especially if it's dust
           you know by name
and flirted with
           ungracefully a time or two:
"Nice shoes. I love those
           strap sandals." Rachel Fuller.
A few
      drunk mourners gasped, a few
                more giggled,
and since I was the one who knocked her loose
I rooted in the kitchen,
        found a broom,

but Johnny

        wrestled the splayed broom from my hands
and slapped the heavy ash and particles
of crushed bone toward the can.

                    "Come on now, Rachel,"
he said, "you

        wild woman you," and weeping,
Johnny stabbed and swatted at the floor
until I found a paper towel,

            wet it,
and mopped

       the last fine dust.

            But what next?
At home I left it on the dresser. A month.
Three months.

       "Throw that revolting thing away!"
my wife said.

      Six months.

           "Why are you keeping it?"
Rachel Fuller. Old possibility.
A little loud.

      Sharp. Quick.

         A little sexy.
But what do I know? I met her at a party,
admired her taut,

       tan calves,

          but praised her shoes,
and thought

      she might have been a little sorry
I couldn't find the sly

       next words to say.
Eight months her ashes challenged me to grieve.

But I kept waiting

               and, as I knew it would,

the magic

        leached away, the awe

                     withdrew,

and I disposed of it, her dust, as we do

almost all

        the dead — even those

                 we loved,

loved utterly —

        because they are sheer dust

and should be honored as the dust they are.

One Threw a Dirt Clod and It Ran

One threw a dirt clod and it ran, and when it paused,
another threw a rock and it trotted out of range,
so they pursued it, lobbing rocks and sticks,
just to see it gallop, which was beautiful,
then to keep it running, but when it stumbled on barbed wire
and broke a front leg and crumpled to its knees, entangled,
one hit it with a tree limb and hit it again. It fell
and they, laughing, ran up and kicked it, jumped away,
ran off, ran back and kicked it, till they could stand beside it,
kicking. They cheered when one of them pried loose
a broken fence post. They fought for the fence post
and took turns swinging it until the tangled beast's
slack ribs stopped pumping, heaving. Gasping for breath,
they stared at one another, dropped the post, the stones, the sticks.
They nudged the huge corpse and waited for it to rise,
to rise and gallop over rutted, fenced-off fields
as if there were no ruts, no mud holes, scrub brush, wire,
so they could follow it forever, weeping and hurling stones.

Wind

Wind shook the dead but not yet fallen leaves.
Wind tugged and plucked and rattled the dead leaves,
the wind entreating *come* and the oak leaves,
already dead, saying *no* to death, *no,*
for that was what the wind through brown leaves was — death —
and I was afraid: maple leaves called *take me*
and the wind took them, and I was fascinated
because it snatched and pulled at me and I said *no.*
I said *no* but I loved its hands on me,
loved its familiar and insistent touch —
the mild inquiring tug at my shirtsleeve,
the sweeping breeze that stood my limp hair straight,
the wind that slapped my red cheeks, stung my eyes,
puffed my pant legs, and ballooned my shirt.
I loved the hard wind, loved it, loved the huge
steps I strode when the wind's muscular hand
clamped on my back and thrust me before it,
its will almost my will, and in its hands
I hated resisting the long wind, which I feared,
so I walked at night to the older parts of town,
where huge oaks hung over houses, soared
across the street and knit together above me,
and I stood in unlit streets on strangers' lawns
so their dark oaks would loom above me also,
moving as hugely as anything I knew
— the sky, the rain, the ocean — with me beneath them
or inside them — which, I wasn't sure;
and the leaves, which longed to be immovable,
flailed, fought — and one by one, fighting, let go

to the wind, the irresistible smooth wind,
and my life, which I had not yet lived,
clung to those oaks and hickories — my life,
my parents', brothers', everybody's lives —
clung to green twigs while the wind was claiming us,
though only I, I thought, only I saw it,
and I kept silent. Perhaps it was a secret.
The vacant limbs, and they were as yet full,
would soon, I understood this, soon leaf out again.
Soon the wind would lift furled yellow leaves,
unfurl them green, and smooth them. Soon the wind
would flood the air with golden dust, warm perfume,
intoxicants of spring that tempt us, tempt us
to run up green hills, roll down them, and forget
the near-percussive thrum, the deep vibration,
half rattle, of brown leaves on brown leaves, the rich
enveloping sound shimmer that haunts the soul
their hymn has summoned, conjured, then cast out,
and they were it, they were my soul because
for the wind we're all the same: already gone,
already gone though we refuse to go —
and the long wind sweeping us away, I longed
to be the wind, which is the deep, untroubled
inhaling or exhaling of our god.
But I was not the wind, or the leaves wholly,
riding without knowing what it was,
the in-breath or out-breath of the Lord,
and as I stood beneath them, listening,
the leaves sang, dying, *Don't die,* and I've obeyed them.

The Daffodils Erupt in Clumps

The daffodils erupt in clumps
so thick they
                lift a block of dirt
above their heads, raising
                              dark soil
in exaltation, offering
wet earth
                to wet March air. The tight
leaves split and sag. The flowerhead
bulls up-
                ward, tilts the lifted earth.
Hard, cold rain
                        bangs the remnant back,
back through tall stalks, earth
                                  to earth,
where it
                belongs, and flowerheads
unfurl their yellow fripperies,
which to us
                are mere loveliness,
though they have work to do, and do it:
honeybee and bumblebee and even moth
ransack and rummage them.
                                  But beauty
unfurled for one eye catches many,
and I
                snip flowers for the table,
where, sipping wine like Nero,
                            pensive,

I'll study them as Nero studied
the corpse of Agrippina,

                    handling
the suddenly compliant limbs,
admiring

           one arm, faulting

                        one.
"I hadn't known," he said,

                  "I hadn't known
my mother was so beautiful."

Elegy for the Bees

At dusk I crouch in greenery and watch the roses
go unplundered, the violets unravished. The chaste
white lily grows more virtuous than ever,
and everywhere I walk, the peonies,
perfumed lasciviously, soften past lush to blowsy, seducing
the bee that isn't there to be seduced
— a sad, unnatural absence in the garden —
the yellow dust untroubled on the stamen,
the pollen ungathered, the seed unmade,
the fruit unformed and therefore never swollen,
not green, not ripe, not plucked and eaten.

Oh, I could stoop over lilies, dabbing
stamen to stigma, anther to pistil, and I do —
a human bumbler in the void,
the swaying limbs and bobbing flowerheads
abuzz with nothing, no ardent bodies
squirming and rooting in the bloom,
ransacking nectar, draped with pollen
like yellow pantaloons, like golden saddlebags.

Each blossom's Rome no longer, for what is Rome
when she has thrown the city gates wide open
and no one enters, and Babylon when she
has pulled down all her seven walls and no one takes her?
And Nineveh, what is she, and what is Egypt
when no one comes to loot the golden dust
with which each empire turns into the next?

Bodies of Water

My shoulder twinges where
his twinges and my left ankle
throbs exactly where
his ankle throbs
and pulses. I look down
and my diagonal
handwriting — angular
and tall — mimics his quick
impossible scrawl slanting
from his hand, his short fingers
clenched on the pen,
and the dry skin of my
right hand is blotched, like his,
with early liver spots.
I'm simply enormous with him,
my whole body full
of him: pink face, bald head,
gray stubble — the same as mine,
the same as his. Small ears
and freckled arms the same —
although my lips are fuller,
my build a little slimmer,
I remind myself. Eyes brown,
not blue. My mother's eyes.
But it's him I'm heavy with,
heavy with my father, heavy
with departure. He's becoming me
so he can leave, and when
I walk near bodies of water

they call to us because
we too are bodies of water.
Ocean and lakes pull,
tug, pluck at us, and from
inside me my watery father
leans toward them, pulls, trying
to break free, pulls fiercely
when I walk by the river:
Ohio, Alabama—
it make no difference; the surge
of huge brown sluggish current
sings, and I hear it singing—
sings to the water shut
in my cells, calling it
to break free — plasma, spittle,
blood, and the various
locked pockets of flux. *Break free,*
it croons and carols, chants
and chortles. *Break free, break free*
— the river's song, death's aria—
and from my cells, my father
sings back inside the choir
of voices he's become,
sings with heartbreaking joy
of his desire, his longing,
his need, need, need
to join the river, yes,
he yearns to be the river,
and like the river (*as*
the river, *is* the river)
he aches for the gulf, the sea,
the ocean — all the time-honored
and time-dishonored metaphors

for birth, death, and rebirth.
I understand that. But this,
this isn't metaphor.
Or not just metaphor:
it is my father's body
inside me singing with joy
to the river's joys, which
are surge, ebb, eddy, flood,
and obliteration. On these
flat pages I too sing,
sing so you will not hear
the sorrow and misunderstanding
I can't hide when I'm talking.
Singing? Is this singing?
I'm trying to sing one song,
not two, one song that's both
my father's song and mine,
writing with (whose is it?)
my familiar, unfamiliar hand.

Babylon in a Jar

Driving home past airport beer joints, I counted
the Sunday drunks passed out beside their cars.
I envied and hated the drunks because my life
was already so ordered and driven by work
that leisure looked romantic to me, romantic
because it was impossible. At work
I sold tickets to rich folks leaving town,
then stood at black glass and watched the midnight planes
turn into lights, accelerate, rise,
and dwindle into darkness and the east —
Atlanta, the world. I didn't want to leave,
I simply wanted to be left alone —
and since that was impossible, I worked
and went to school and worked some more,
and there those drunks lay, nestled in the gravel
and oystershell, half-buried and asleep,
while I sped by, sleepy myself, but sober.
I've never talked so elegiacally
about myself, and I dislike the bland
forgiveness of it — as if I were beyond
the night wind's buffeting and the day wind's bite,
as if from my great height of understanding
I'll fade into my death, never afflicted
with greater suffering than I can bear.
It feels so much like wisdom to talk this way.

I finished school and because I was now married
I kept two jobs and sometimes, briefly, three.
Late Sunday afternoons, my wife and I

sat on the porch, talking and watching bright water
arc into the air above our yards and our neighbors',
then fall as measured rain. Children shouted.
Gunshots and laughter wafted from nearby windows:
the television world — always violence,
and exaggerated laughter, which I loved.
The perfume of seared meat rose from our grills.
Ice clicked in cheap gin, and now and then it cracked,
a solitary explosion in our hands.
They weren't what I was living for, those moments.
Perhaps they should have been. I cannot now
regret the squabbles and quick capitulations
of young lovers striving to be dignified,
to be *noble,* inside their earnest striving.
How glibly elliptical these abstractions are!
I'm simply using grand words for the pleasure
of pronouncing on myself, and to build
a walkway to my new life. But what life is new?
It's the same good life, still mine, but with
 — there's only one way to say this — a better wife,
good gin, and children that for all I know
could be the same ones playing down the street,
the same dogs barking in the distance. Not
a different life. A better life. Only shorter.
What summit have I now attained that I
watch the young me and the person I now am
ascend together the frozen slopes below my banner?
A sip of gin, the scent of roasting meat
and the whole disordered world resembles order.

Driving to work, I think of those distant drunks,
not with the rage I felt when I was young,
but gently. I want to lie down next to them

on pea gravel and oystershell still warm
with the day's heat, and burrow into it
and dream someone else's dreams. Then I'd drive home
and face the consequences. What? I don't know.
I can't imagine. But dreams and memories
have consequences, and when I think of those drunks,
those sleeping drunks, night work, that distant city,
I remember how Sennacherib quieted the heart
of Ashur, his bitter Assyrian god:
he obliterated Babylon. He burned it —
Babylon, that vast metropolis, that great city.
He razed the charred buildings, slaughtered the few
remaining people, but before he flooded the rubble,
he swept up the dust of Babylon
to give as presents, and he stored it in a jar.

How to Stop

Through the cracked door I saw
                    the jeweler's fine,
white,
        rapid fingers
                    flit above my watch.
His head dipped once or twice and then the woman
— his wife, his sister, or the hired help:
                            who knows? —
brought back my watchband, one
                    link shorter,
                            fixed.
"Thanks. What do I owe you?"
                    The woman glanced
back toward the dead man, who didn't raise his head
or turn around.
            "Forget it," he called.
                        "Hey, thanks!
Hey, thanks a lot," I said. Two or three bucks
was breakfast, lunch,
                and supper to me then.

Last week I named him from the radio,
and in the paper I first saw his face,
long
        and sad,
                as if he knew some thug
would kill him for a wedding ring.

"But why'd you have to shoot him?" the cops asked.
"I don't know, man.

                      I just did. Okay?"
"Forget it," Tommy Posey told me — advice
from a man who had done me a kindness. Brightened
my day, as Hallmark says.

But now that I have begun to talk about him,
how do I
          stop? I could mention
                    my watchband
was now, in fact, too tight, and pinched red welts
into my wrist. Or I could tell you
                 the killer
said, "Look, I want to put all this behind me
and get on with my life." Or
             I could muse
on Tommy Posey as a link removed,
leaving shadowy
        what he had linked
               to what —
because I cannot penetrate the shadows.
Or I could
       point out I'm paying off a debt,
or trying to. I could
         shrug my shoulders,
the way I do, when
         after a drink or two
I tell this story to appall a friend.
I could go on
       forever, trying to stop.

There is no reason for stopping.

      You just stop.

But leave that good name hanging in the air:

Tommy Posey,

    who'd done me a kindness when I needed one.

In Alesia

In Alesia, our last town, our final stronghold,
we sent our women and our children out.
When Caesar sent them back, we, to feed our warriors,
we let them starve outside the walls of Alesia.
Our men fought well but not as well as Caesar's,
and in Alesia our handsome king conferred on us a choice:
You may kill me or deliver me to Caesar.
We could not kill him. Outside the breached walls of Alesia,
our broken stronghold, we delivered him to Caesar,
and we watched him throw himself down before Caesar, surrendering,
and we heard Caesar speak coldly to him, our handsome king,
and we saw him bound in chains. With scornful clemency
Caesar dismissed us. For a long time we heard nothing.
We plowed our charred fields, using each other as oxen.
Some of us found new gods, and some of those gods were Roman.
We paid our grain levies and, when he demanded them,
we sent our sons to Caesar and he made them soldiers.
In Alesia, we fathered new children and smiled sadly,
remembering our first children, first wives, our handsome king,
and then, in Alesia, we heard they'd kept him caged six years,
six years in a cage, our handsome king, our famous warrior,
six years before they dragged him through their capital,
some gray barbarian from some forgotten war, our handsome king,
our well-nigh savior, a relic of an old war six years settled.
We heard they tortured and beheaded him, his head
jabbed on a pike and left till it fell off —
as we have ourselves, from time to time, honored the Romans.
We wish now we had killed him, our handsome king —

embraced him, kissed him, killed him, and buried him in Alesia.
If we were Romans, yes, we could have killed him,
and if he were Roman, he'd never have made us choose.

Rain

It's raining women here in Cincinnati.
Parts of women, parts of one woman?
The police aren't really sure. Last week
they found an arm, a leg, another arm,
and at eleven last night, while I sipped
the meticulously measured
good bourbon of my middle age,
reporters blandly announced the torso,
no horror in their voices — a slight
professional hush to show they're human too
and they're affected by what they tell us.
Not too much, of course. TV is not
the place for outrage, those coifed homunculi
appropriate for weather, sports — nothing
more tragic than lost football games. Let us
save outrage for our private lives.
(Though isn't this my private life?)
Let the family that has not, as yet, missed her
live outraged. For me, it's pity and terror,
then off to bed unpurged of them,
to seek catharsis in my nightmares. There
the search continues. How can we bury her,
the human jigsaw scattered, half lost, half found?

Like the student who rushed up after class,
I thought we'd passed beyond the ancient myths.
"That stuff you said? About the olden times,
blood sacrifice and fate?

That was true then. It's not true anymore,
is it?" She was almost sobbing.

Listen,
my undivided sum, unsundered darling,
listen: Attis, Adonis, Christ, Osiris,
the flute player, the cropped green ear of corn,
whom butchery has transformed into gods;
and this poor slaughtered housewife, whore, hitchhiker,
whom we cannot make whole, though we must try.
Fate. Blood obligation. They're in the news.
We live them every day.

But I said, "No,
it's not true anymore. We aren't all Isis.
We won't all be Osiris."
She smiled. I smiled. She wiped her tears.
Let living teach her what it has to teach her.
She's young. American. Let her resist.
But let the red dismembered gods safeguard
her unsevered flesh. Let those whose work it is
die for her and be scattered on the planet:
God's Scavenger Hunt, God's Hide-and-Seek, God's Tag,
You're It. Amputate, then sew. Explode,
then gather. Smash, repair.
Like a small boy with a radio or frog,
we hack and reassemble our old unmurderable gods
so we won't tear each other into pieces.

Eternity's a ball, history is a stick.

Ball

Nose down, she
            courses the back yard, searching
for her ball
       until she sniffs it,
               hidden
in tall grass. She pivots on her nose
and vectors in on it,
          from base
to apex
      of a frantic triangle,
her brown tail's white tip spinning
               like
a rotor. She finds it, snatches it,
and lopes in a long arc back to me.
As much as finding it,
          she loves
to hold it in her soft mouth,
            wriggling
with the pleasure of being a retriever
retrieving.
      Pure essence, bred to it.

When I think of beauty,
          I think of this
dog stretching to
        full stride, long
loose muscles undulating underneath
brown fur,
       until she's running
           too fast,

misjudges, smacks her ball
                       into the neighbors'
magnificent azaleas, and scrabbles through them,
too focused on the zigzag ball
to ponder
            dignity, the sublime,
or love, and thus attaining them —
the body fully body till it drops,
exhausted.
             Tongue lolling on brown grass,
she stares at me,
               alight
with the exacting genius of her joy.

Keys

Freed
          from my winter coat, giddy
                              with sunlight
gauzy through greening limbs, I pitched my keys
into honeysuckled
                    air, higher and higher
and higher — toss,
                    snatch, toss — until
they snagged the power line.
                              Neck craned,
I glared at them,
                twelve feet
                              above my face.
I cursed. I stomped around my suddenly
unyielding house.
                    I rattled both doors
and pried at all
                five windows. I'd locked them
against the world. Now
                        they were locked on me.
I threw an oak limb at the dangling keys,
missed, threw again,
                        for twenty timed minutes — then
the stick
          struck perfectly. The keys
bucked from the line.
                        My house was mine again!
But first I stepped clear of the power line

and hurled bright keys

                  into bright air and caught them

— once overhead and once behind my back —

before I slapped the steel

                  key in the lock,

kicked

        the oak door open, and sang

                        "I'm home,

I'm home" into the sun-invaded hall

the front

        door breached, the windows at my mercy.

When the Weak Lamb Dies

When the weak lamb
                    dies, the shepherd skins
the body, stretches
the skinned fleece like a little lamb suit
over an abandoned lamb,
                              the lamb's
front legs
          jammed through the front leg holes
and the back legs jammed through the back
                                        leg holes —
the live lamb wrapped in the loved scent
of the dead one, and
                      the deceived ewe lets
the orphan suckle.
                  Within a day,
when he begins to shit her milk
and she smells his shit and smells herself,
he's hers.
          This is what the dead
are for: for use, hard
                        use, the duped
ewe giving suck and the orphan lamb
sucking more
              than he can swallow, milk
pouring down his chin, chest, legs,
soaking
        the straw and packed dirt,
                                    flooding

back into his closed eyes, splashing the ewe —
a blessing so huge it looks like waste
as we choke,

   gag, gulp, gag,

      gorge ourselves.

Tools: An Ode

The cheap
        screwdriver reams the cheap
                screwhead,
and the dull blade burns white oak and splinters cherry.
The loose wrench
        torques the bolt on crookedly
and strips the thread. But guided by good tools,
the screw bites freely to its full length,
              the board
rips cleanly,
        and the hex nut weds its bolt.
Thin shavings rise in long unbroken curls,
each lovely in itself.
        The good tool
           smoothes
rough lumber underneath the unforced hand,
unwarps
        the warped board, trues
           the untrue edge
before it chops the mortise, cuts the tenon,
and taps them home
        in happy marriage. With good tools
the edge falls
        plumb and all
           four corners square.
The house holds snug against the crashing wind,
and there
        is order in the polity
and pleasure in the handmade marriage bed.

The Hanging Gardens

Gone: The Palace of Forty Columns. Gone:
The Garden of Heart's Ease, The Garden of Roses.
Gone: The Garden of the Shah. And even
The Garden of the Throne is nothing now
but rubble unreflected in brown rain
drying in the ruined reflecting pool. Gone,
the hanging gardens built for a homesick queen
who missed the meadows of her childhood mountains.

A child pondering my old *Book of Wonders,*
I daydreamed of gardens floating over the desert
in never-ending bloom — green steppingstones,
each lush with lilies and bromeliads.
I thought they were wizardry, not work,
in the dry land of tamarisk and camel thorn.
Amytis knows. And doesn't want to know.
The gardeners hide from her. The cypresses
are lovely, yes, and the waterlilies too —
lovely the date palms lining the waterways,
and the blooming water hyacinths — but I,
because I'd read my *Book of Wonders,* knew
their purpose was to shade the channeled water.

As Amytis at nightfall ascends her garden,
turning tier on tier in the cooling dusk
in the present tense of our imagining,
she doesn't touch the waterlilies. They'll part,
uncovering the lead-lined troughs — reeds, tar.
Through gaps in ivy and purple clematis,

she sees and doesn't see the slaves' palm prints
fired in rough brick. Beside the river, she'd watched
young slaves slap wet clay into bricks, then pile
dry brush on them. Before they lit the piles,
one slave — she'd seen him and she hadn't seen him —
strolled the haphazard rows, pressing his palms
into the soft brown river clay and twisting.
(I've seen him do this. Why can't Amytis?)

Down the false mountain, dammed, channeled, pumped
Euphrates water cascades like a mountain stream,
murmuring like a mountain stream, purling
and chuckling over artful, moss-draped stones,
but when she isn't careful Amytis hears
the shaduf's splash and creaking, laden rise.
If her mind drifts, she'll hear the steady clomp,
the muted huffing of the ox against its yoke,
the capstan's squeal, the slip and drag, the rasp
and slop of chain pumps forcing water up the mountain.
Freed, it plunges, rippling like a stream,
shaded with ferns, protected by blue cedars,
and, along the streambed, cultivated moss
is painted with spoiled milk and brushed like velvet.

All planned: each brown bloom plucked and carried off,
and every barren spot is soon adorned
with a new rarity: white myrtle, rosy
oleander with its almond scent,
narcissus, bonarets from Scythia —
a thoughtful gardener calculating her
bedazzlement.
                    Impatiently, she prowls
the rooftop garden of her upmost terrace,

watching the blurred red sun disintegrate
and slide below the crenellated walls
of her dry kingdom. The first stars separate
from the harsh sunlight overdazzling them,
and her eyes open and she begins to see
what she has come to see.

She ascends an artificial mountain, descends
an otherwordly garden. Each paradise
adores its wolf, its snake, its scorpion.
She savors possibility: assassins
beneath the roses, demons in the willow.
Now, anything can happen, although it never does,
and I, a torchbearer, arise from the tall grass,
ignite my torch, and join the path. She follows.
The upward path is now the downward path,
and on the way down — backward, dark — black leaves,
wind-lashed in flaring torchlight, lunge at us,
beat at their twigs. And when the leaves rip free,
pelt toward us, tangle in her hair, she laughs
and lets them stay — laughs, and follows me.
But not me really, and not the torch,
but torchlight as it slides
across white blossoms, changing them to moons —
blue, luminous, and unattainable:
torchlight and nothing. An ache for paradise,
says my new *Book of Wonders,* pages filled
with new research and fresh equivocation
spilling from the past and past-perfect tenses:
a pile of dubious rubble in the desert.
A name that may have been a mistranslation.
A garden that was built by another, later king
for a concubine. Or wasn't built at all.

Or that was, at best, a mound of mud
planted with short desert trees and brush.
And through the wavering possibilities
I see her and I do not see her walking
the rectilinear spiraling ziggurat
uphill at dusk, downhill in moonlight;
walking through her own absence; picking her way
discreetly through rubble in the desert; circling
a mound too closely planted for her to climb;
walking the rectilinear spiraling ziggurat,
uphill at dusk, downhill in the moonlight
of a word Herodotus misunderstood.
Or understood. I see her and I do not see her.

From

ECSTATIC IN THE POISON
(2003)

In

When we first heard from blocks away
the fog truck's blustery roar,
we dropped our toys, leapt from our meals,
and scrambled out the door

into an evening briefly fuzzy.
We yearned to be transformed —
translated past confining flesh
to disembodied spirit. We swarmed

in thick smoke, taking human form
before we blurred again,
turned vague and then invisible,
in temporary heaven.

Freed of bodies by the fog,
we laughed, we sang, we shouted.
We were our voices, nothing else.
Voice was all we wanted.

The white clouds tumbled down our streets
pursued by spellbound children
who chased the most distorting clouds,
ecstatic in the poison.

Beneath the Apple

The house atilt with laughter, jazz,
and tipsy friends, I eased
into the yard, and took a breath
of dark, chill evening, pleased

to leave behind smoke, drink, and noise.
I lumbered to the apple
in the darkest corner, near the fence,
and underfoot, a windfall,

crushed to paste, infused the air,
its sweetness lush with rot.
(I ought to take it down, the apple.
But that's an afterthought.)

Too much to drink and my house full,
I leaned against the tree
and stared back into yellow windows,
perplexed — why now? — to see

my friends, whose lives I know too well
and who know mine. We share
long histories but decreasing time.
We make good laughter bear

what laughter can, which is a lot.
I saw my smiling wife
finger an old friend's bright new hair
and risk an honest laugh.

A hundred feet away in darkness —
and I knew what she'd said
and what her laughing friend said back,
her hair a fevered red.

I leaned into the teeming tree,
fumbled, and emptied myself
onto its peeling bark. The dog
strolled over, took a sniff,

and emptied himself too — two mammals
depositing their salts
against the boundary tree. I named
and then unnamed my faults

as I stood under unplucked fruit —
a spiteful woodland god,
I thought. Or tried to think. The god —
or was it I? — guffawed.

I sauntered up the lawn in joy,
a ghost. Nothing was mine.
The house, the friends, the night. I loved
that moment: Dead. Divine.

The Ship Made for Burning

For ten days while he was in the ground
we women sewed rich garments for him.

                                          We men
drank night and day and made for him a ship
made for burning, and we asked his girl slaves,
"Who will die with him?"

                     and I said, "I,"

and we two attendants groomed her and washed her feet.

What did you do when your father left the earth?

And I who am the slave girl drank and sang,
and gave myself to leisure.

                             When the ship was made,
we removed the lord's corpse from the earth. We dressed him
in soft boots, a caftan studded with gold buttons,
and we propped him on a cushion in the ship
and surrounded him with meat, his blades, his dog.
We each lay with the slave girl and we each said,
"Tell your master I've done this for love of him."

What did you do when your mother left the earth?

I made that vow to each man as he left me.
They raised me over the doorframe and I said,

"Behold, I see my mother and my father,"
and they lowered me and raised me again and I said,
"I see my ancestors seated at the feast,"
and they lowered me and raised me again and I said,
"I see my master seated in Paradise
and Paradise is beautiful and green.
He calls me. Take me to him."

What did you do when your brother left the earth?

They carried me into the pavilion with my master
and, thick with sweet beer, I lay against his chest
as I had lain when he was yet alive,
though never for an entire night, never receiving
the whole of his great warmth, not being his wife,
but neither was I his body slave, she
who merely washed his gray hair, cooked his meat,
and scraped the day's sweat from him. I bore him children.

What will the living do when you pass on?

And we strangled her and stabbed her and burned the ship
made for burning, launched it on red waves,
and we drank as it burned down to cinder and ash,
beyond the reach of insects, and we raised a birch post
and wrote the name of the Rus king on it, and we departed.

The Cadillac in the Attic

After the tenant moved out, died, disappeared
 — the stories vary — the landlord
walked downstairs, bemused, and told his wife,
"There's a Cadillac in the attic,"

and there was. An old one, sure, and one
with sloppy paint, bald tires,
and orange rust chewing at the rocker panels,
but still and all, a Cadillac in the attic.

He'd battled transmission, chassis, engine block,
even the huge bench seats,
up the folding stairs, heaved them through the trapdoor,
and rebuilt a Cadillac in the attic.

Why'd he do it? we asked. But we know why.
For the reasons we would do it: for the looks
of astonishment he'd never see but could imagine.
For the joke. A Cadillac in the attic!

And for the meaning, though we aren't sure what it means.
And of course he did it for pleasure,
the pleasure on his lips of all those short vowels
and three hard clicks: the Cadillac in the attic.

Southern Literature

She hunched in the back seat, and fired
one Lucky off the one before.
She talked about her good friend Bill.
No one wrote like Bill anymore.

When the silence grew uncomfortable,
she'd count out my six rumpled ones,
and ask, *noblesse oblige*, "How ah
your literary lucubrations

progressing?" "Not good," I'd snarl. My poems
were going nowhere, like me — raw,
twenty-eight, and having, she said,
a worm's-eye view of life. And awe —

I had no sense of awe. But once
I lied. "Terrific! *The Atlantic*
accepted five." She smiled benignly,
composed and gaily fatalistic,

as I hammered to Winn-Dixie, revving
the slant six till it bucked and sputtered.
She smoothed her blue unwrinkled dress.
"Bill won the Nobel Prize," she purred.

If I laid rubber to the interstate
and started speeding, how long, I wondered,
how long would she scream before she prayed?
Would she sing before I murdered her?

Would we make Memphis or New Orleans?
The world was gorgeous now, and bigger.
I reached for the gun I didn't own.
I chambered awe. I pulled the trigger.

The Chinaberry Trees

. . . and oh, the chinaberry trees in niggertown!
—E. WELTY TO K. A. PORTER, 1941

Under the flowering chinaberry,
we parked, and drifted on the tide
of hot scent ebbing toward a dream
we shied from. Mystified,

we gave ourselves to fragrance, eyes shut
to barrel fires, and wicks
flickering in smoky shacks.
What was there to fix

our eyes on — purple flowers hidden
in the leaves and the leaves in darkness?
We didn't have to understand
what we had witnessed. Fragrance

numbed and suspended us among
then-the-past and then-
the-future, and then, which was the now
we levitated in.

I've never been so far transported,
as I was there, under trees
I wouldn't have on my green lawn.
By May, the fetid berries

rot in the hot shade underneath
the lowest branches. Crows
riot in the reeking poison,
not harmful to them of course —

shrieking like Furies in the fruit,
mating and making mess.
Azalea, redbud, cherry grace
our lawns. And our success

drove us, March nights, past barbecue
and juke joints. We parked outside
tilted shotgun shacks, eyes closed,
and breathed deep, nullified,

releasing ourselves to perfume, knowledge
out of context, abstraction
our talking couldn't dim. We lived
in the pilfered Indian

gift of the chinaberry — the tree
uprooted from my lawn
but thriving there in niggertown,
lush and left alone.

When a gray battered truck scraped past,
we awakened, blinking. Once,
thrilling us, a pistol shot rang out,
and after, in the silence,

a raw harmonica exploded,
someone's ridicule

sucked backward through the instrument,
the laughter lurid, cruel,

and magnified to frightening music —
except we weren't afraid
or chastened. We reveled in its rage,
and hung on its harsh fading.

The White Horse

Unswerving, neither graceful
nor ungraceful, running at
the absolute last limit
of its power, a white horse
pounds across the desert
and without pausing plunges
down a cliff, its hind legs pumping
left, right, blasting clouds
of dust, its legs and chest
dyed red with dust. It's tearing
straight through me like a spear.
Why am I not screaming?
No. It hammers past,
red hooves churning wild grass,
which flies, and with the red dust
settles on my hair, my shoulders.

Stop. I'm sorry. I was afraid.
Restart the vision.
                    Horse
rockets down torn red cliff
and I step in front of it.
It hits me, kills me. No,
absorbs me, and we are running
across the red desert,
running at the absolute
new limit of our power,
gaining speed, our white
face shadowed like a skull,

our cheeks hollowed with pure
velocity. Join us.
                Make us faster, faster,
O faster . . .

Come to Harm

We were driving from one state to another,
my father already there,
and we'd been singing hymns, hymns
soaring from the car

with our joy at passing on to glory,
where loss would turn to gain,
our wounds would heal — and in the silence
after our last refrain

my mother said she'd known, known
before the call had come,
her father had died. She'd felt his passing.
She'd known "He'd come to harm" —

as if Death had enticed him. As if
he had returned to drinking
and wed Death's hootchie-cootchie girl,
Death's crude seducer. Thinking

"True Tales of the Supernatural!" I wondered
how I could tell this story
and make friends shudder. Or failing that,
— I was this predatory —

how I could make them laugh. I flipped
"There's a world beyond this world"
to "My mother is a silly woman" —
and back again, as we hurled

through darkness singing songs of hope.
She told her sacred story.
We sang. We laughed. She died. I wept.
Her story isn't mine. I'm sorry

— and not — about how I have told it.
Who knows what's coming after?
There may be another world. There may.
There will be laughter.

The God of Frenzies

The tall boy shook and shimmied across lunch tables,
shouting at us to shout.
"Jeez, what a jerk," I thought, but I still shouted.
I couldn't stop myself.
Strapped to his torso, pinned up and down his legs,
blue pompoms snapped and sizzled. We screamed with him,
and as we roared, he rode
our screaming, swam in it like water, soared.
We shook our pompoms at the living pompom,
and — mad, ecstatic — he
burst into flame. The boy inside the flames
froze one half-second as he changed
from flesh to fire. He raced
across the tables, and leapt toward us. I thought
it was stagecraft, part of his act.
Who would have thought that what looked true was true?
I couldn't hear his screams above our screaming.
I couldn't see him flopping on the floor.
Later we heard a story:
a match flipped at the swirling paper. A joke.
Though I know now that I was seeing terror
— a boy burning on a table —
I remember joy, the boy flung gratefully
to his full blazing length onto the air
as if he thought the air would hold him.
At that false remembered moment,
I saw terror and ecstasy,

and I would ask the god of frenzies why
with both choices before him, he chose terror,
though I know there was no reason. He simply chose.

Behemoth and Leviathan

"Can you draw out Leviathan
with a fishhook?" Yahweh sneers.
We have drawn out Leviathan.
At first with terror, then cheers,

and then the grunted curse of work.
We've hunted him to nothing.
We drawn him with a fishhook, Lord,
and then we've stilled his thrashing.

We've locked Behemoth in a pen
for children — and his horn
we've ground for an aphrodisiac.
We've plucked it like a thorn.

Earth-shakers wallow in zoo mud
and every morning amble
to their steel troughs and wait for food,
hungry but hugely gentle,

and the great ship-destroyer sits,
a jar of yellow oil
in a bright museum in Salem, where
I saw myself recoil

and gag at ancient rancid fat.
We've drawn his mighty tooth
and etched it with the memories
of his efficient death.

Deep is shallow, distant close,
the predator defended,
the fierce incomprehensible
now fiercely comprehended.

But in their looming disappearance
they're what they've always been:
Behemoth and Leviathan,
and chaos at the margin.

Beatitudes

Blessed is the Eritrean child,
flies rooting at his eyes for moisture. Blessed
the remote control with which I flipped on past.
Blessed the flies whose thirst is satisfied.
Blessed the parents, too weak to brush away
the vibrant flies.
                    Blessed the camera crew
and blessed the gravity of Dan Rather, whose voice
grows stranger with every death he sees. Blessed
my silence and my wife's as we chewed our hot
three-cheese lasagna.
                    Blessed the comedies
we watched that night, the bed we slept in, the work
we rose to and completed before we sat
once more to supper before the television,
a day during which the one child died
and many like him. Blessed is the small check
we wrote and mailed. Blessed is our horror.

In the Cool of the Evening

Among lilies I am Jehovah,
the Lord God walking in the cool of the evening,
delighting in every green that grows, sorrowing
for those that fail. I am Christ the healer:
I spray for black spot and white fly, pluck aphids,
and when the leaves turn crisp I pluck them too
and drop them in the dirt to soften and return.
The Lord God walking in the cool of the evening.

With books I am merely the student,
saying why, why, why — exasperating myself
and even the long-dead with my questions.
But among dianthus, I am the decider:
Not here, but there. Not you, but something else.
The Lord God walking in the cool of the evening.

Beside bellflower, poppy, phlox, I keep the deathwatch.
Among lilies I am the slow mourner for the soft bulb
rotting in damp clay, the quiet griever
over fire blight in the pyracantha — fire blight,
canker, scale — and when I fail as Christ, I succeed
as the adversary, root-digger, extirpator —
the Lord God walking in the cool of the evening.

Beyond branch tips, where they scrape the sky,
I see the sheets are white, starched, and my skin is yellow,
yellow and going gray. Down the row,
the Lord God walks in the cool of the evening,
delighting, sorrowing, healing, failing to heal.

I am very calm, I am almost not afraid.
I look neither toward him nor away from him,
the Lord God walking in the cool of the evening.

The Fourth Year of an Eight-Year Drought

Let us consider the Carthaginians.

Let us consider the Carthaginians
entering the fourth year of an eight-year drought.

Blown sand scours the granary's inside walls.
Sand
      rattles in the empty oil pots, and rakes
the dying groves. Sand frolics in the well.

Let us consider the Carthaginians
as they examined their lives, and sacrificed.

Swaying to the rhythmic
               clash of tambourines,
drums, trumpets, they march the length of their dry city.

Let us imagine we're Carthaginians.
Let us imagine we march through our dry city.

To drown the wailing we would never wail,
bell-ribbons
         snap above our heads. We kiss
and tickle, tease and pet our fretful infants
so they'll be laughing, legs
              kicking with delight
when the priest pulls the knife across their throats.

Let us imagine willing sacrifice.

We offer them to the god like lambs or bulls,
which have not

        pleased the god. Our tiny souls
unfold when, singing, we lay our firstborn sons
in the god's bronze arms.

            No one sobs or moans.
No one taints the sacrifice. No one
begrudges

      the first lamb, first

             dove, first

                 peach, first
full bushel of summer grain — the dearest offering
inadequate

      for rain, wheat, and the sons,
whose elders, sacred warriors, saved our city.

Let us understand we live in Carthage.
Let us understand our sacrifices.
It is the fourth year of an eight-year drought.

Land of the White Crows

The people there are much like us,
he said. In war, they're brave, he said.
Like you. And he broke off a crust
and speared a slab of yellow fat.
But the people over there, he said,
sleep on bare ground. For ornament,
a man there wears an iron collar,
and tethered to it by a chain
a crow sits on his head. The crows,
he said, the crows are solid white.
White crows! In our puzzled hush he grabbed
the goat's foreleg and pulled it free.
He chewed as we debated white crows.
One white crow is a marvel, easy
to comprehend. But a flock of crows
the color of a flock of swans
disturbs the words we use for words.
Do white crows still eat carrion?
And how, if crows are white, could we
sing the old songs, describe the night?
He filled a horn with our good cider.
Could coal be white? Could snow be hot?
Since he passed through two springs ago,
we cannot stop debating crows
or the hungry stranger at our fire
who, with white crows, transformed our world
to air, then wind, as he passed through
from somewhere strange to somewhere strange.

Wasps in August

With the death craze on them, wasps in August
rage near their paper nests,
defending them from raccoons, jays,
and other ravening guests

that hunger for the feast — and risk
the deathwatch wrath of wasps.
They'll swarm on anything to save
the spit-and-tissue wisps,

their soft spawn pulsing as they swell.
And in their common need
to gorge the hardening larvae in the nest,
they stand and bleakly feed

on broken apples in the yard.
They don't pause, don't buzz, don't
fly up in fear and light again.
They simply stand and eat,

then ferry nectar to the nest.
Death calls, and they're replying,
The nest, the nest, the nest, the nest.
The easy job is dying.

A Joke Walks into a Bar

A joke walks into a bar and takes a pun
  — a ten-inch pun — out of his pocket. He orders
a beer. The pun kicks it into his lap.
Another beer. The pun dumps it. Amazed,
the barkeep laughs, then whispers to the joke:
"Hey, Mack, where'd you get him?"

                          And suddenly
the joke was tired. He no longer cared to talk
about the witch, or how — young, dumb, and drunk —
he'd begged for a ten-inch prick. He sighed, paid,
and left the bar, the pun still racing up
and down the counter, kicking over drinks.

The joke sold his whoopee cushions, rubber chicken,
even his Bozo shoes. And the next time
his left foot hit a black banana peel,
he didn't hang suspended in midair,
but fell. A broken coccyx, fractured skull.
In pain, he drank, groaned, drank, cursed, drank, and, drunk,
exposed himself to incurious schoolgirls,
groped boys in public restrooms. Nothing helped:
somebody somewhere will laugh at anything —
a hair between your teeth, a sore that's shaped
like Florida, a child that screams exactly
like a scorched parrot when some drunk strokes his bottom.

The joke washed, shaved, joined six A.A. groups,
the Methodist church, and the Rotary Club.

But he kept slipping back to desert islands.
Whorehouses. Church. For hours he sat on barstools,
drinking Coke and questioning his friends.
He wanted to know what happened to the chicken
once it had crossed the road. Did it stay there?
Did it go back? Or was the chicken locked
into an endless cycle of road crossing
and recrossing because the side he'd left
was now the other side? The chicken didn't know,
and the joke felt cruel for asking. Old steps he'd danced
so elegantly now felt like old steps. He was,
he thought, like an aging playboy at a brothel.
He wanted the fat madam to sit near him
and tell him how much fun he used to be
when he was young and flush.
                              As he left the brothel,
the April wind whipped his hat from his head.
It tumbled down Main Street, and he remembered
how, all his life, he'd chased it, the hat his master,
everyone cheering the hat. He stood and watched,
till the wind gave up and swept his tempting hat
into the river. He turned and walked toward home,
and halfway home, alone, he started laughing.

The Long Ship

Death's settled in my suburbs: weak ankles
just a little weaker and the fingers of my right hand just
a little more like unoiled hinges in the cold.
Death's moved into my right shoulder as a flame.
I tease it, taunt it, test it: Can I carry wood?
Can I still throw the ball? How far and for how long?
What's the new price? Higher, but not too high.

Death, darling,
                    you've been gentle up till now.
But after the first kiss I return, we know
how your seductions go: each tender kiss
a little coarser. Each night a little further:
caress to rough insistent stroke. Each qualm
and modest scruple brushed aside till metaphor
gives way to metamorphosis — from one
hard, lived cliché to one nobody lives:
Death's built his long ship, he's raised his black
sail over me, and what ship doesn't love
a steady wind, and what ship doesn't love the white
wake curled behind it like lilies on a black stem.

Piss Christ

Andres Serrano, 1987

If we did not know it was cow's blood and urine,
if we did not know Serrano had for weeks
hoarded his urine in a plastic vat,
if we did not know the cross was gimcrack plastic,
we would assume it was too beautiful.
We would assume it was the resurrection,
glory, Christ transformed to light by light,
because the blood and urine burn like a halo,
and light, as always, light makes it beautiful.

We are born between the urine and the feces,
Augustine says, and so was Christ, if there was a Christ,
skidding into this world as we do
on a tide of blood and urine. Blood, feces, urine —
the fallen world is made of what we make.
He peed, ejaculated, shat, wept, bled —
bled under Pontius Pilate, and I assume
the mutilated god, the criminal,
humiliated god, voided himself
on the cross, and blood and urine smeared his legs —
the Piss Christ thrown in glowing blood, the whole
and irreducible point of his descent:
God plunged in human waste, and radiant.

Blur

Storms of perfume lift from honeysuckle,
lilac, clover — and drift across the threshold,
outside reclaiming inside as its home.
Warm days whirl in a bright unnumberable blur,
a cup — a grail brimmed with delirium
and humbling boredom both. I was a boy,
I thought I'd always be a boy, pell mell,
mean, and gaily murderous one moment
as I decapitated daises with a stick,
then overcome with summer's opium,
numb-slumberous. I thought I'd always be a boy,
each day its own millennium, each
one thousand years of daylight ending in
the night watch, summer's pervigilium,
which I could never keep because by sunset
I was an old man. I was Methuselah,
the oldest man in the holy book. I drowsed.
I nodded, slept — and without my watching, the world,
whose permanence I doubted, returned again,
bluebell and blue jay, speedwell and cardinal
still there when the light swept back,
and so was I, which I had also doubted.
I understood with horror then with joy,
dubious and luminous joy: it simply spins.
It doesn't need my feet to make it turn.
It doesn't even need my eyes to watch it,
and I, though a latecomer to its surface, I'd
be leaving early. It was my duty to stay awake
and sing if I could keep my mind on singing,

not extinction, as blurred green summer, lifted
to its apex, succumbed to gravity and fell
to autumn, Ilium, and ashes. In joy
we are our own uncomprehending mourners,
and more than joy I longed for understanding
and more than understanding I longed for joy.

Out

My father cinched the rope,
a noose around my waist,
and lowered me into
the darkness. I could taste

my fear. It tasted first
of dark, then earth, then rot.
I swung and struck my head
and at that moment got

another then: then blood,
which spiked my mouth with iron.
Hand over hand my father
dropped me from then to then:

then water. Then wet fur,
which I hugged to my chest.
I shouted. Daddy hauled
the wet rope. I gagged, and pressed

my neighbor's missing dog
against me. I held its death
and rose up to my father.
Then light. Then hands. Then breath.

Acknowledgments

I am grateful to the editors of the following publications in which some of the poems in this collection first appeared:

DoubleTake: "Epithalamium."
The Georgia Review: "The Afterimage of a Ghost."
The Hopkins Review: "Accelerator."
The Hudson Review: "Cicada," "The Names of the Lost."
The New Criterion: "Courtesy," "Outside the Inn," "Walking a True Line."
Poetry: "After Teaching," "Blowfly," "My Daughter."
River Styx: "American Rendering."
Salmagundi: "Lorraine's Song."
Slate: "Lightning Strike in Paradise."
The Southern Review: "Came Back."
TriQuarterly: "Abandoning the Play," "The Circus."

"Mother" first appeared in *Surreal South: An Anthology of Short Fiction and Poetry,* edited by Laura and Pinckney Benedict and published by Press 51 in Winston-Salem, North Carolina.

The Overlook Press generously granted me permission to include poems from *Ecstatic in the Poison* (Overlook Press, 2003), and for that I owe special thanks to Peter Mayer and Juliet Grames.

I am grateful to the Guggenheim Foundation for a fellowship during which many of these poems were written, as well as to the Ohio State University and the Ohio State University College of Humanities for grants that provided invaluable time to complete the book. My agent, Marianne Merola, has been a staunch and adroit advocate. I am indebted to good friends whose astute criticism, advice, and encouragement have made me a better writer than I would have been without them: the late Peter Davison, Mark Jarman, Ellen Voigt, Michael Collier, Wyatt Prunty, and my wife, Erin McGraw.